Biography Today

*Profiles
of People
of Interest
to Young
Readers*

Volume 17
Issue 3
September 2008

Cherie D. Abbey
Managing Editor

*P.O. Box 31-1640
Detroit, MI 48231-1640*

Cherie D. Abbey, *Managing Editor*

Peggy Daniels, Joan Goldsworthy, Jeff Hill, Kevin Hillstrom, Laurie C. Hillstrom,
Eve Nagler, and Diane Telgen, *Sketch Writers*

Allison A. Beckett and Mary Butler, *Research Staff*

* * *

Peter E. Ruffner, *Publisher*
Matthew P. Barbour, *Senior Vice President*

* * *

Elizabeth Collins, *Research and Permissions Coordinator*
Kevin M. Hayes, *Operations Manager*
Cherry Stockdale, *Permissions Assistant*

Shirley Amore, Martha Johns, and Kirk Kauffman, *Administrative Staff*

Copyright © 2008 Omnigraphics, Inc.
ISSN 1058-2347 • ISBN 978-0-7808-1018-1

The information in this publication was compiled from sources cited and from
sources considered reliable. While every possible effort has been made to ensure reli-
ability, the publisher will not assume liability for damages caused by inaccuracies in
the data, and makes no warranty, express or implied, on the accuracy of the information contained herein.

This book is printed on acid-free paper meeting the ANSI Z39.48 Standard. The infini-
ty symbol that appears above indicates that the paper in this book meets that standard.

Printed in the United States

Contents

Preface

Biography Today is a magazine designed and written for the young reader—ages 9 and above—and covers individuals that librarians and teachers tell us that young people want to know about most: entertainers, athletes, writers, illustrators, cartoonists, and political leaders.

The Plan of the Work

The publication was especially created to appeal to young readers in a format they can enjoy reading and readily understand. Each issue contains approximately 10 sketches arranged alphabetically. Each entry provides at least one picture of the individual profiled, and bold-faced rubrics lead the reader to information on birth, youth, early memories, education, first jobs, marriage and family, career highlights, memorable experiences, hobbies, and honors and awards. Each of the entries ends with a list of easily accessible sources designed to lead the student to further reading on the individual and a current address. Retrospective entries are also included, written to provide a perspective on the individual's entire career.

Biographies are prepared by Omnigraphics editors after extensive research, utilizing the most current materials available. Those sources that are generally available to students appear in the list of further reading at the end of the sketch.

Indexes

Cumulative indexes are an important component of *Biography Today*. Each issue of the *Biography Today* General Series includes a Cumulative Names Index, which comprises all individuals profiled in *Biography Today* since the series began in 1992. In addition, we compile three other indexes: the Cumulative General Index, Places of Birth Index, and Birthday Index. See our web site, www.biographytoday.com, for these three indexes, along with the Names Index. All *Biography Today* indexes are cumulative, including all individuals profiled in both the General Series and the Subject Series.

Our Advisors

This series was reviewed by an Advisory Board comprising librarians, children's literature specialists, and reading instructors to ensure that the concept of this publication—to provide a readable and accessible biographical magazine for young readers—was on target. They evaluated the title as it developed, and their suggestions have proved invaluable. Any errors, however, are ours alone. We'd like to list the Advisory Board members, and to thank them for their efforts.

Our Advisory Board stressed to us that we should not shy away from controversial or unconventional people in our profiles, and we have tried to follow their advice. The Advisory Board also mentioned that the sketches might be useful in reluctant reader and adult literacy programs, and we would value any comments librarians might have about the suitability of our magazine for those purposes.

Your Comments Are Welcome

Our goal is to be accurate and up-to-date, to give young readers information they can learn from and enjoy. Now we want to know what you think. Take a look at this issue of *Biography Today*, on approval. Write or call me with your comments. We want to provide an excellent source of biographical information for young people. Let us know how you think we're doing.

Cherie Abbey
Managing Editor, *Biography Today*
Omnigraphics, Inc.
P.O. Box 31-1640
Detroit, MI 48231-1640

editor@biographytoday.com
www.biographytoday.com

Congratulations!

Congratulations to the following individuals and libraries who are receiving a free copy of *Biography Today*, Vol. 17, No. 3, for suggesting people who appear in this issue.

Miranda Becker, Danville, ID

Jessica Blanchard, Aboite Elementary, Ft. Wayne, IN

Michael Bosquez, San Saba, TX

Janis Brooks-Owings, Robyler Middle School, El Reno, OK

Amanda Heidecker, Marysville, WA

Mary Louise Helwig-Rodriguez, Little Falls Public Library, Little Falls, NJ

Hallie Mazzanera, Hartmenie School, Salt Lake City, UT

Alberto McCley, Sulphur Springs, TX

Alexis Pedretti, Magnolia Elementary, Riverside, CA

Brianna Watson, Clarksboro, NJ

Tiana Watson, Philadelphia, PA

Diego Yangali, Valley Stream, NY

ALY & AJ

Aly (Alyson Renae Michalka) 1989-
AJ (Amanda Joy Michalka) 1991-

American Singers and Actresses

BIRTH

The singing and acting team of Aly and AJ is made up of two sisters: "Aly" is Alyson Renae Michalka, who was born on March 25, 1989, and "AJ" is Amanda Joy Michalka, who was born on April 10, 1991. Both were born in Torrance, California, and they spent the early years of their life in that city, which is part of the greater Los Angeles area. Their father, Mark Michalka, is a commercial contractor. Their mother, Carrie

Michalka, is a musician who has played in a Christian band and other musical groups and previously worked as a cheerleader for the Los Angeles Raiders football team.

YOUTH

Both Aly and AJ inherited their mother's love of performing, and they took to the stage at a very young age. Their first "shows" took place around the time when Aly was five years old and AJ was three. They put on dance routines for friends and relatives and also sang and appeared in plays at their church. Soon, they began attending acting workshops and studying piano. "It just came naturally to them," their mother said of their musical abilities. "It wasn't forced at all." The girls later took up the guitar and became skilled at that instrument as well. From the beginning, they liked to perform together, which reflects the close relationship they have always enjoyed. Aly and AJ have described themselves as "the first set of twins to be born two years apart," and their bond is a key part of their musical collaboration. "Aly and I are best friends," AJ explained. "Working together means I can basically hang out with my best friend all the time." Aly has agreed with that idea, noting that the few sisterly disagreements they have are short-lived because "we never stay mad at each other for long."

> "
>
> *Aly and AJ have described themselves as "the first set of twins to be born two years apart." As AJ explained, "Aly and I are best friends. Working together means I can basically hang out with my best friend all the time."*
>
> "

The Michalkas moved to Woodinville, Washington, while Aly and AJ were young. It was there that the sisters first began appearing as models for print advertisements and magazine photographs. Those jobs, along with their appearances in plays and musical shows, made it clear that they possessed a great deal of talent and a strong desire to launch serious professional careers. The only holdup was their parents, who worried that the demands of show business might cause the girls to miss out on some important parts of growing up. "They really wanted us to live normal lives," AJ explained in the biography *Amped Up: Aly & AJ.* "That was what they were weird about, in a good way." In the end, however, mom and dad decided to let their daughters pursue their dream.

EDUCATION

Even after becoming professionals, Aly and AJ still had to devote time to their education. They had been home-schooled throughout their lives, however, so they were able to adopt a flexible schedule that helped them to fit their assignments in around their other work. Both girls graduated from an independent-study charter school—Aly in 2006 and AJ in 2007—and were the valedictorians of their respective classes. The sisters are interested in attending college, though they have no definite plans on where or when they will enroll.

CAREER HIGHLIGHTS

Though fans of Aly and AJ's music may think of the girls as an inseparable team, the two started out by pursuing individual modeling and acting careers, and both became successes in those fields before being signed to a record deal. The first to strike gold was AJ, the younger sister, who began modeling around age nine. She landed jobs in print advertisements for Disney and American Girl and also appeared in national television commercials. AJ was eager to take on dramatic roles, and her career got a boost when the Michalkas left Washington and moved back to the Los Angeles area, where many TV shows and movies are produced. She made her breakthrough in 2002, appearing briefly on a daytime drama and then landing the part of the Huntress on the WB series "Birds of Prey," which was cancelled after 13 episodes. Roles in other TV programs followed over the next two years, including a continuing part as Shannon Gressler on the CBS drama "The Guardian."

Meanwhile, Aly was also working hard to establish herself as an actress. In 2004, her efforts paid off big time when she won the leading role on the Disney Channel series, "Phil of the Future." Aly played Keely Teslow, the best friend and love interest of the title character, Phil Diffy. The show proved a huge hit with young viewers and remained on the air for two seasons. "'Phil of the Future' was how I got known," Aly said. "What a way to start out your career, being part of such a great big company that is so successful and is really able to launch you."

Breaking into the Music Business

That "great big company" is Disney, which has helped launch the careers of Hilary Duff, Miley Cyrus, and several other performers, who found stardom as actors and also as recording artists. Aly and AJ were very interested in this kind of dual career because they had continued to work on their music even as they became successful actresses. "Music is what we love the most," Aly declared. "With music, it comes from your heart and soul. It's all you."

Aly & AJ performing onstage at a Christmas concert.

Hoping to land a label contract of their own, the girls recorded a tape of their material and gave it to executives at Hollywood Records, which is part of the Disney Music Group. Both the tape and a live audition wowed company executives, and Aly and AJ were offered a recording contract.

Soon after signing on the dotted line, they entered the studio to record their debut album.

Into the Rush was released in August 2005, when Aly was 16 years old and AJ was 14. The album immediately caught the attention of the so-called 'tween market—young people roughly between the ages of and eight and 14. AJ has described her and Aly's music as "pop with a whole lot of melody," and a catchy, upbeat sound was a big part of the album's appeal. That was especially true of the first single, "Do You Believe in Magic," a tune that originally was a hit 40 years earlier. The duo also won a lot of fans with another "cover" song, "Walking on Sunshine," which was first recorded in the 1980s.

Becoming Songwriters

There was more to Aly and AJ's music than re-recording feel-good numbers that had been written by others, however. They also revealed themselves as prolific songwriters. In fact, the sisters helped write 12 of the 14 songs on *Into the Rush*, collaborating with their mother and other musicians to create the compositions. This kind of hands-on involvement in the creative process is unusual for young artists who are still in their teens, and it helped give the album a personal tone that won the approval of a number of reviewers.

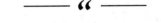

"Music is what we love the most," Aly declared. "With music, it comes from your heart and soul. It's all you."

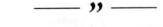

Even more unusual was the fact that the girls didn't confine themselves to such topics as relationships or enjoying fun times with friends. Instead, they used certain songs to explore more serious topics. "Sticks and Stones" talked about the dangers of bullying, while "I Am One of Them" discussed the topic of kidnapping. "It's not just about boys and having the perfect day," Aly said, commenting on the duo's music. "Sometimes it's nice to listen to a song that makes you think."

Aly and AJ's mix of infectious music and thoughtful lyrics was a hit, and the CD went gold, meaning that it had sold more than 500,000 copies. They took to the concert stage soon after the album was released and proved that they were accomplished live performers. After a successful 2005 tour opening for the Cheetah Girls, they received top billing for their 2006 performances, and even had the honor of performing an Easter concert at the White House. In the fall of that year, they released the holiday-themed album *Acoustic Hearts of Winter,* which included two original songs along with versions of Christmas favorites.

Following the recipe for success that had been created by other Disney artists, Aly and AJ kept themselves in the spotlight by appearing in TV programs even as they won greater acclaim for their songs and concerts. Aly had a lead role in the Disney made-for-TV movie *Now You See It* in 2005, which featured "Do You Believe in Magic" as part of its soundtrack. Both girls co-starred in the Disney's *Cow Belles* in 2006, where they played two spoiled sisters who are forced to take an active role in running their father's dairy operation.

——— **"** ———

Aly & AJ consider themselves role models for their young fans, and they pick their acting roles accordingly. "We want to make sure it's something we can show our kids when we get older," AJ explained. "We have a standard we want to set— and that means not doing anything we don't believe in."

——— **"** ———

Setting a Good Example

Aly and AJ understand that their fame makes them role models for thousands of young people, and they take that responsibility very seriously. When considering acting roles, they choose projects that they feel send a proper message. "We want to make sure it's something we can show our kids when we get older," AJ explained. "We have a standard we want to set— and that means not doing anything we don't believe in." The sisters followed these guidelines even before they became well known, with AJ once refusing to take part in a scene on the TV show "The Guardian" that she felt was questionable.

The girls' responsible attitude stems from the values they learned in the Christian church that their family attends. While spiritual devotion is central to their lives, the sisters choose not to be overtly religious in their songs. "We don't ever want to preach or shove anything down people's throats," Aly explains. AJ has similar thoughts and adds that too strong of a religious message might alienate some listeners. "We don't want to exclude anybody," she said. "If we have a Muslim fan or an atheist fan, that's their thing—I'm gonna love them no matter what." At the same time, the girls do believe that Christianity has an influence on their art. "There is a sense of unconditional love that AJ and I have," Aly observed. "It helps with our songwriting because there's no pressure—to write a hit or to

Some of their early work—their first CD, Into the Rush, *and a scene from the movie* Cow Belles.

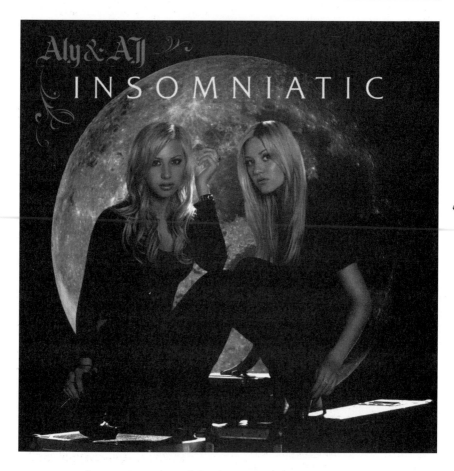

Insomniatic *showed the duo's maturing musical tastes.*

write certain things. There's a certain calm and peace our faith brings us. We can write about anything."

Using their fame to benefit good causes is another priority for the duo. Their concern about the issue of child abduction led them to become co-chairs of the AmberWatch Foundation, which works to prohibit kidnapping. In addition, they served as the 2007 spokespersons for the Samsung Hope for Education program, which provides technology products to schools.

Insomniatic

When Aly and AJ began work on their third CD, they decided to try a new approach. "On the next album we want to have a little more rock and try to mix things up," AJ said in 2006. By seeking a more powerful sound, they were moving closer to the style of some of their favorite bands, which include two groups that were popular in the 1980s: Heart and The Police.

Once finished, the album *Insomniatic* hit the stores in July 2007. The duo's new direction ended up incorporating not only more rock elements but also a dance-oriented sound, with "Potential Breakup Song" and "Like Whoa" emerging as the initial hit songs. Lyrically, the album focused on romance, exploring both the excitement of new relationships and the disappointment of seeing them end. In both style and subject, the sisters were appealing to an older audience, which was sensible, given that many of the former 'tweens who had bought their first record were now well into their teenage years. Aly put it in simple terms: "We want our fans to grow up with us, not outgrow us." *Insomniatic* received generally positive reviews, and listeners seemed to like what they heard. The album debuted at No. 15 on the national charts, and steady sales will likely make it the sisters' second gold album.

Several other projects also brought Aly and AJ a lot of publicity. About the time that *Insomniatic* was released, they were also featured in the MTV movie *My Super Sweet 16*, a fictional story inspired by the reality TV show of the same name. In the movie, two best friends since childhood (played by AJ and Regine Nehy) are planning an extravagant, shared sweet-16 party. Then a third girl (played by Aly) steps in and drives them apart, and soon the two former best friends are competing to see who can put on the most outrageous party. Aly and AJ also received a lot of exposure from various promotions and products that were unveiled in the summer of 2007. They appeared on Honeycomb cereal boxes, and their concert tour was sponsored by Sanrio, with the company designing a special "Hello Kitty" tour bus for the occasion. In addition, a long list of Aly and AJ licensed products began to appear on store shelves, including video games, apparel, jewelry, cosmetics, dolls, and more. There is even a book series, Aly & AJ's Rock N Roll Mysteries, which features the young singers' adventures on tour as they solve

——— " ———

"There is a sense of unconditional love that AJ and I have," Aly observed. "It helps with our songwriting because there's no pressure—to write a hit or to write certain things. There's a certain calm and peace our faith brings us. We can write about anything."

——— " ———

mysteries. Two volumes have been published to date: *First Stop, New York* and *Mayhem in Miami.*

Aly and AJ have proven themselves to be masters of merchandising and cross promotion. But they find the greatest satisfaction in creating and performing quality music, and they have put a lot of work into achieving that goal. "[Some people] look at our music as some kind of formula. Like we're just actresses trying to be singers," noted Aly. "But we've both loved music since we were little. It's much more than just going up there and singing. It's a lot of blood, sweat, and tears." She also believes that most listeners find real substance and meaning in their songs. "People are starting to realize that we're more than just some pop band," she declared, "[that] we're songwriters with a real message."

HOME AND FAMILY

Aly and AJ reside with their parents in Calabasas, California. They have four dogs, Saint, Bandit, Roadie, and Willow.

HOBBIES AND OTHER INTERESTS

When they're not working, Aly and AJ try to lead fairly quiet lives. "We are normal girls who just happen to act and sing," AJ said. They tend to avoid parties and other high-profile gatherings and instead seek out quiet time away from the celebrity hubbub. "We really value just relaxing," Aly explained. "Every kid—even if you're not in the business—definitely needs to find time to chill and do nothing." Outdoor activities are important to both girls. They spend a lot of their spare time boating, water-skiing, swimming, mountain biking, and riding horses, though they also greatly enjoy the indoor "sport" of shopping.

SELECTED CREDITS

Recordings: Aly and AJ

Into the Rush, 2005
Acoustic Hearts of Winter, 2006
Insomniatic, 2007

Television Programs: AJ

"Birds of Prey," 2002-2003 (TV series)
"The Guardian," 2003-2004 (TV series)
Cow Belles, 2006 (made-for-TV movie)
My Super Sweet 16, 2007 (made-for-TV movie)

Television Programs: Aly

"Phil of the Future," 2004-2006 (TV series)
Now You See It, 2005 (made-for-TV movie)
Cow Belles, 2006 (made-for-TV movie)
My Super Sweet 16, 2007 (made-for-TV movie)

FURTHER READING

Books

Norwich, Grace. *Amped Up: Aly & AJ*, 2007 (juvenile)

Periodicals

Billboard, June 16, 2007, p.7
Girls' Life, Apr./May 2008, p.34
Los Angeles Times, June 23, 2007, p.E16
Today's Christian, Jan./Feb. 2007, p.52
Tulsa World, July 7, 2006
USA Today, July 6, 2007, p.D3

Internet Articles

http://www.billboard.com
    (Billboard, "Aly & AJ Writing New Songs, Plot Films," Jan. 10, 2008)
http://www.discoverygirls.com/entertainment/celebrities/aly-aj-star-sisters
    (Discovery Girls, "Aly & AJ: Star Sisters," no date)

ADDRESS

Aly & AJ
Hollywood Records
500 South Buena Vista Street
Burbank, CA 91521

WORLD WIDE WEB SITES

http://www.alyandaj.com
http://www.myspace.com/alyandaj

Majora Carter 1966-

American Urban Planner, Environmental Activist, and Advocate for Environmental Justice
Founder and Executive Director of Sustainable South Bronx

BIRTH

Majora Carter was born on October 27, 1966, in New York City. She was the youngest of ten children born to her parents, Major and Tinnie Carter.

YOUTH

In the 1940s, Carter's parents moved to the New York City neighborhood known as the South Bronx and began raising a family there. As the years passed, though, the South Bronx underwent a grim transformation. "When my parents moved there in the '40s," Carter explained, "it was this mostly white working class community and this was [my parents'] first step up the economic ladder." In the 1950s and 1960s, however, many white families moved to the suburbs. Banks and other financial institutions also abandoned the neighborhood. The poor residents who were left—mostly African-American and Latino families—had little economic or political power. As a result, their neighborhood became an industrial dumping ground. By the 1970s, the South Bronx was lined with abandoned factories, crumbling warehouses, and waste treatment plants. Its streets were mostly used by drug dealers, prostitutes, and diesel-powered trucks that polluted the neighborhood air.

> "I watched half of the buildings in my neighborhood burn down," Carter recalled. "My brother Lenny fought in Vietnam only to come home and be gunned down a few blocks from our home. I grew up with a crack house across the street. Yes, I'm a poor black child from the ghetto."

It was hard for Carter and her older siblings to grow up in this setting. "I watched half of the buildings in my neighborhood burn down," she recalled. "My brother Lenny fought in Vietnam only to come home and be gunned down a few blocks from our home. I grew up with a crack house across the street. Yes, I'm a poor black child from the ghetto."

As she grew older, the misery and poverty that surrounded Carter also took a toll on her self-image. "When everything you see is dirty and ugly, it's hard not to have it reflect on you," she explained. "As a kid, you never fully understand what makes that sort of thing happen, but it teaches you that you're probably not worth much."

Fortunately, Carter had a strong foundation of support to lean on during her childhood years. As she later said, she was able to lift herself to a better life thanks to the "love inside [her] home" and the "encouragement of teachers, mentors, and friends along the way." Still, when she left her neighborhood to attend college, Carter felt grateful at the thought of leaving the South Bronx behind. "I left and vowed never to return," she admitted. "It did not seem to present any kind of livable opportunities."

EDUCATION

Carter attended elementary school in the South Bronx. She earned excellent grades, which enabled her to gain admission into the Bronx High School of Science, one of the best public schools in the city. She graduated from the school in the spring of 1984.

A few months later, Carter enrolled at Wesleyan University in Middletown, Connecticut. "The older folks were just pleased as punch and super proud that I was in college, period, that I didn't become a statistic, that I wasn't pregnant at 14 the way many of my friends were," she said. Carter made many friends at Wesleyan, but she admits that few of her friends knew much about her background. Since she was ashamed of her old neighborhood, she always spoke vaguely when friends asked her about her childhood. "The South Bronx was the poster child for urban blight for many, many years and I hated it," she said.

After graduating from Wesleyan with a bachelor's degree in cinema studies in 1988, Carter spent the next few years trying to decide what she wanted to do with her life. She eventually settled on the idea of going back to school. She returned to New York City, and in 1997 she earned a master's degree in English from New York University.

CAREER HIGHLIGHTS

In order to obtain her master's degree, Carter did something that she had vowed that she would never do: she moved back into her childhood home in the South Bronx. She intended to stay only a short time. Carter reasoned that temporarily moving in with her parents would enable her to save enough money to finish graduate school. She also thought that her parents' loving presence might help her deal with the emotional bruises she had acquired from a very brief marriage that had just ended in divorce. "I returned because there was nowhere else to go," she later acknowledged.

During her first weeks back in the South Bronx, Carter felt moments of great regret. The grim warehouses, trash-strewn lots, and dangerous alleyways depressed her, as did the roaring parade of diesel trucks and the stink of the sewage treatment plants. But little by little, her feelings of hopelessness gave way to anger about living conditions in the community. With a growing sense of duty to her old neighborhood, she became a program director for a small arts-related community development organization.

A short time later, Carter made her first forays into political activism. "One day I heard about the mayor's plan to privatize waste handling in the city," she recalled. "They were going to shut down the Staten Island landfill

*Carter has long been involved in public outreach,
talking to community members about social issues.*

without any environmental review and divert the waste handling to our neighborhood. I thought, 'Wait, we already handle 40 percent of the city's commercial waste, and that would bring in another 40 percent of the city's municipal waste.' As I researched, I began to realize that if we're not actively meeting the environment needs of our community, then all the art in the world isn't gonna help."

It was around this time that Carter decided to take action. She did not want to see the next generation of South Bronx kids "grow up in such a toxic environment," so she decided "I would like to be part of something that actually makes life better for people as opposed to doing nothing." With that in mind, she launched a grassroots campaign to derail the city's plan to build yet another waste facility in the South Bronx.

"Mobilizing the community wasn't easy," Carter admitted. "I think we had been so demoralized and dejected—people knew that this was a forgotten place—that it was hard at first to inspire interest and hope." But Carter did not give up. Instead, she patiently approached community groups, church organizations, and ordinary residents and asked them to join the fight. The people of the South Bronx rallied to her side, and in 2000 more than 700 of them showed up at a public hearing to register their objections to the city's plan. A short time later, city officials quietly dropped the idea.

Reclaiming the Riverfront

Carter's next crusade was triggered by the curiosity of a stray dog that she had rescued from the streets of the South Bronx. After finding the dog on the street, she took it home and named it Xena, after the television series about a warrior princess. Before long the two were fast friends. Carter even took the dog along for companionship when she went jogging. On one of these morning excursions, Xena made an amazing discovery. "She pulled me into what I thought was another illegal dump," Carter recalled. "She kept dragging me through weeds and other garbage … and lo and behold at the end of that lot was the [Bronx] river. I knew this forgotten street end, just like my abandoned dog that brought me there, was worth saving. And just like my new dog, this idea got bigger than I had ever imagined."

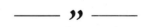

"Mobilizing the community wasn't easy," Carter admitted. "I think we had been so demoralized and dejected—people knew that this was a forgotten place— that it was hard at first to inspire interest and hope."

The sight of the river reminded Carter how warehouses, waste facilities, and other industrial buildings had transformed the South Bronx over the previous decades. Like many other residents, Carter had practically forgotten that the Bronx River even ran past her neighborhood. But after she and Xena returned home later that morning, she began thinking about ways to re-establish the neighborhood's relationship with the river.

Carter decided that the answer was a new riverfront park. She knew that the cost of buying property, removing garbage and abandoned buildings, and building a park would be enormous. But she did not let these obstacles stop her. Instead, she lobbied tirelessly for private donations and grants from nonprofit organizations and government agencies. Little by little, Carter found the necessary money, and in April 1999 the Hunts Point Riverside Park opened to the public. "People were out on the water in canoes and kayaks," she recalled. "They were saying, 'Wow, oh my gosh, there's water here.' It was a very beautiful moment."

Carter and local young people at the opening of the Riverside Park.

According to Carter, the opening of the park also triggered an important change in community attitudes. "It was one of those life-changing moments," she said. "We asked, 'What do you want to see within your community?' It was very empowering to folks who had never been asked what they wanted."

Sustainable South Bronx

The triumphant opening of Hunts Point Riverside Park launched Carter down a new career path as an urban planner. Inspired by her success with the park, she established a nonprofit organization called Sustainable South Bronx in 2001. The goal of this organization, she explained, was to further improve the lives of the people of the South Bronx by creating jobs, reducing local pollution, and expanding "green space"—trees, parks, and other natural surroundings—within the city. "Poor communities of color are just as deserving of clean air, clean water, and open space as wealthier ones," she declared.

Over the next few years, Carter launched a wide range of SSBx projects to help the people of the South Bronx. She designed a community waste reduction program and sponsored "Greening for Breathing," a neighborhood-wide effort to plant trees and other greenery. Carter even collaborated with Columbia University and the City University of New York (CUNY) on an air quality study of the neighborhood. This study confirmed that the South Bronx was saddled with very high levels of local air pollution, which has been widely blamed for causing high rates of asthma among South Bronx children.

In addition, Carter established a successful job training project for the community called the Bronx Environmental Stewardship Training (BEST) Program. The BEST program takes area residents and trains them for careers that protect and restore the urban environment in which they live. "We recruit folks, almost exclusively from the neighborhood," Carter said. "I'd say 95 percent have been on public assistance, and most just received their GEDs [high school General Equivalency Diplomas]. The ages range from about 20 to 45 and we train them in everything from landscaping and green-roof installation to brownfield remediation [cleaning up urban areas contaminated by pollution]." According to Carter, most graduates of the BEST program immediately move into paying jobs.

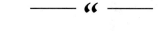

"Poor communities of color are just as deserving of clean air, clean water, and open space as wealthier ones," Carter declared.

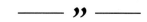

Carter is especially excited about so-called "green-roof installations" as an environmentally smart job creator. She even launched a company, SmartRoof, to install and maintain green roofs around the city. Green roofs are not a reference to color, but rather to their environmental character. These flat roofs are covered with thin beds of soil that sustain wild flowers, native grasses, and strawberry and blueberry plants. Green roofs provide additional insulation for buildings, which cuts energy use. They also absorb rainwater, which reduces the volume of runoff that city sewage plants must process. Finally, they provide welcome sanctuaries of color and life in this urban setting.

Champion of Environmental Justice

All of the Sustainable South Bronx programs that Carter has launched over the years reflect her deep belief in "environmental justice." According to Carter, this term means that "environmental benefits and burdens [should be] equally distributed among all people, and ... not determined by race or class." As she noted in a 2007 speech, though, the United States is far away

Carter at the installation of a green roof, an environmentally friendly approach to building construction.

from reaching this goal: "Right now, it is race and class that are excellent indicators of where you will find the good stuff like parks and trees and where you'll find the bad stuff like waste facilities and power plants and dead-end jobs that degrade the environment and, by the way, lead to such things as really high asthma rates and obesity and diabetes."

According to Carter, the path to greater environmental justice lies in "creating opportunities for people to enjoy the environment around them, which means the environment needs to be something that can *be* enjoyed. It needs to be supportive of people's health and their economic quality of life." She also believes that environmental justice is only possible if all people—not just the wealthy or politically connected—are given a voice in shaping the world around them.

Many people in the South Bronx report that Carter's voice has already made a big difference in their lives. "The neighborhood has done a 180-degree turn," said one resident. "Trees are coming in, people are keeping the streets cleaner. There are new stores—all these things have made living here a lot better." Another resident who works for SSBx declared that the foundation's success in greening the community "gives me hope for the future."

A National Leader

The efforts of Carter and her Sustainable South Bronx organization have attracted national attention as well. In 2005 she received one of the most famous awards in the United States—a MacArthur Fellowship, also known as a "genius" grant. These awards are given annually by the John D. and Catherine T. MacArthur Foundation, an organization that is "dedicated to helping groups and individuals foster lasting improvement in the human condition." To do this, they identify individuals whose creativity and past accomplishment suggest a successful future. The foundation praised Carter as a "relentless and charismatic urban strategist" who is "profoundly transforming the quality of life for South Bronx residents." The award includes a grant of $500,000 over five years, enough to allow the winners the financial independence to pursue further creativity.

—— " ——

"The neighborhood has done a 180-degree turn," said one South Bronx resident. "Trees are coming in, people are keeping the streets cleaner. There are new stores—all these things have made living here a lot better."

—— " ——

Carter's public profile has risen in other areas as well. She has played a leadership role on a number of New York state environmental councils, and she was keynote speaker at the 2006 National Business for Social Responsibility Conference. Carter is also a member of The Clinton Global Initiative's Poverty Alleviation Panel, a philanthropic organization founded by ex-president Bill Clinton. Her work has been praised by such diverse magazines as *Newsweek,* which named her to its 2007 list of 25 to Watch, and *Essence,* which named her to its list of the country's 25 Most Influential African Americans. Finally, Carter has received prestigious awards from such respected environmental organizations as the National Audubon Society and the Natural Resources Defense Council.

The effective work carried out by SSBx is the most obvious reason for Carter's meteoric rise to prominence. Close observers say that the accomplishments of Sustainable South Bronx are a direct result of her bold personality. Carter refused to be intimidated by corporate lawyers, city bureaucrats, powerful lawmakers, or wealthy philanthropists. Instead, she showed spirit, determination, and confidence in her dealings

Carter at her desk at Sustainable South Bronx.

with everyone she came across. "She is as comfortable chatting with world leaders as she is training single mothers and returning felons who are reentering society to care for shade trees or build green roofs on energy-efficient buildings," concluded Bracken Hendricks in *Apollo's Fire.*

Carter has also refused to let the awards and attention distract her from her goals. In 2008, in fact, she achieved a long-time SSBx priority when the city of New York began construction of the South Bronx Greenway. When completed, this Greenway will include 11 miles of cycling and walking paths extending from the heart of the South Bronx community to the Bronx River waterfront. And Carter continues to raise millions of dollars to clean up areas of blight in the South Bronx—and block other polluting businesses and facilities from entering the community.

Urging Others to Get Involved

In her travels around the United States, Carter often speaks with journalists, lawmakers, and community organizers. But she also makes a special effort to reach people who are living in depressed urban surroundings. "My dream is that others will do what we've done in their own communities," she observed. "Do something that gives back to your community, whether it's writing to your representative in Congress about an environmental issue or volunteering at a neighborhood park clean-up." Carter believes that once people get involved in community issues, they often discover leadership skills that they did not even know they had. "A successful leader is somebody who follows the needs represented by the population," she stated. "Everybody has the capacity to be a leader. It's just stepping up to the plate when something has to be done."

Carter also urges people who live in comfortable suburban homes and neighborhoods to show greater compassion for those who are less fortunate. "I see so many women getting worked up about polar bears, when in reality every city has its own South Bronx, where greenhouse-gas sources have been affecting people for decades," she said.

MARRIAGE AND FAMILY

Carter was briefly married in the mid-1990s, but that marriage ended in divorce. She then remained single until October 2006, when she married James Burling Chase, a communications specialist. The couple exchanged wedding vows at Hunts Point Riverside Park. "He's one of the most stabilizing and funny forces in my life," said Carter.

HOBBIES AND OTHER INTERESTS

Carter's work with Sustainable South Bronx keeps her very busy, but when she does get a break she likes to go camping, snorkeling, and roller-skating. She also enjoys reading and home renovation. "One day I'd like to write a screenplay for a movie," she adds, "but I don't have the time now."

SELECTED HONORS AND AWARDS

Environmental Quality Award (U.S. Environmental Protection Agency): 1999

Union Square Award (Fund for the City of New York): 2002

Women's History Month Pacesetter Award (New York City Council): 2004

MacArthur Fellowship (John D. and Catherine T. MacArthur Foundation): 2005

Earth Day Environmental Advocates' Award for Achievements in Community Development (Natural Resources Defense Council): 2006

Rachel Carson Women in Conservation Award (National Audubon Society): 2007

Martin Luther King Jr. Award for Humanitarian Service (New York University): 2007

FURTHER READING

Books

Inslee, Jay, and Bracken Hendricks. *Apollo's Fire: Igniting America's Clean-Energy Economy,* 2008

Kerry, John, and Teresa Heinz Kerry. *This Moment on Earth: Today's New Environmentalists and Their Vision for the Future,* 2007

Periodicals

Chicago Tribune, Nov. 12, 2007

Christian Science Monitor, Oct. 31, 2007, p.13

Chronicle of Philanthropy, Oct. 27, 2005, p.44

Essence, Jan. 2005, p.24; Dec. 2007, p.207

Jet, Oct. 10, 2005, p.36

New York, Feb. 26, 2007, p.26

New York Times, Dec. 3, 2000, p.C1; Aug. 15, 2001, p.B2

Newsweek, Dec. 25, 2006, p.68

PCMA Convene, Dec. 2006, p.79

Shape, Nov. 2007, p.168

Online Articles

http://www.outside.com
   (*Outside,* "Green All Stars: Community Leader," Apr. 2007)
http://www.plentymag.com
   (*Plenty Magazine,* "A Bronx Tale," Feb. 13, 2007)
http://www.quickandsimple.com
   (Quickandsimple.com, "The Queen of Green," undated)
http://www.vibe.com
   (*Vibe,* "Majora Carter: The Green Thumb," Aug. 8, 2007)
http://www.grist.org
   (*Weekly Grist,* "Majora League," Sep. 28, 2006)

ADDRESS

Majora Carter
Sustainable South Bronx
890 Garrison Ave., 4th Floor
The Bronx, NY 10474

WORLD WIDE WEB SITE

http://www.ssbx.org

Anderson Cooper 1967-

American Television Journalist
Host of the CNN News Show "Anderson Cooper 360"

BIRTH

Anderson Hays Cooper was born on June 3, 1967, in New York City, New York. His father was Wyatt Emory Cooper, a screenwriter who hailed from a poor farming family in Mississippi. His mother was Gloria Morgan Vanderbilt, a famous socialite and fashion designer. She was an heiress to the family fortune built by her great-grandfather, railroad tycoon Cornelius Vanderbilt. Cooper had one older brother, Carter, who committed suicide in 1988.

YOUTH

Cooper grew up in a luxury apartment building in Manhattan, in New York City. Such famous individuals as Andy Warhol, Charlie Chaplin, and Truman Capote were frequent dinner guests. According to Cooper, though, his parents created a home environment that kept him from becoming spoiled or snobbish. "Neither of my parents believed in joining clubs or being involved in anything that reeked of elitism or exclusiveness," he recalled. "Growing up, 'elitist' was the worst thing you could say about someone."

Instead, Cooper's parents encouraged him to be independent and curious about the world around him. "What was cool about my parents was, my brother and I were expected to sit at the adult table," he said. "There was never a kids' table. To me, the greatest privilege of the way I grew up was realizing at a very young age that these [famous] people are just as unhappy as everyone else. Once you realize that, it frees you up from believing that fame or riches are going to bring you happiness. I think it takes a lot of people a long time to figure that one out." These conversations also helped him understand that successful people did not have all the answers when they were young, either. "It was comforting to me when I figured out that you don't have to know what you want to do with your life; you just have to take a few steps in one direction, and other opportunities will open up."

> "*Neither of my parents believed in joining clubs or being involved in anything that reeked of elitism or exclusiveness," he recalled. "Growing up, 'elitist' was the worst thing you could say about someone.*"

In other respects, Cooper had a normal childhood. He spent countless hours playing with his brother, who was two years older. "He created giant battlefields for war games with our toy soldiers," Cooper remembered. "The rules were too intricate for me to follow, but I loved to sit and watch him direct armies across the sweeping plains of our bedroom floor."

Like countless other youngsters, Cooper also loved watching television. "I've been addicted to TV since I emerged from the womb," he admitted in a 2006 interview. "I recently found a schedule I made for myself in fourth grade, which was all blocked out based on the TV schedule.... I think I allotted 15 minutes for dinner, and homework was done in front of the tele-

Anderson Cooper (left) running down a street in New York City with his mother, Gloria Vanderbilt, and his brother, Carter Vanderbilt Cooper.

vision. News was always on the schedule as well. I had a reading problem when I was a kid, so writing came a little slow."

In fact, Cooper had dyslexia, an inherited neurological condition in which the reader's brain has difficulty processing letters and words in the proper order. People with dyslexia have trouble recognizing and decoding words, which can make reading and spelling difficult. As a result, they often have trouble with reading comprehension. Cooper's parents hired a special reading instructor to help him deal with it. The instructor's guidance was an important factor in his ability to deal with his disability. "One way she helped was to encourage me to find books that I was really passionate about," he recalled. "I remember reading a biography of Helen Keller and a book about people who chose to live in the woods. Eventually, I read *Heart of Darkness* [by Joseph Conrad]. That novel, in particular, sparked an interest in seeing what happens to society when everything is stripped away, when you're living without the niceties of modern culture."

> "To me, the greatest privilege of the way I grew up was realizing at a very young age that these [famous] people are just as unhappy as everyone else. Once you realize that, it frees you up from believing that fame or riches are going to bring you happiness. I think it takes a lot of people a long time to figure that one out."

Cooper's curiosity also extended to other, distant parts of the world. As a child, he kept by his bedside a miniature globe that had been given to the family by Isak Dinesen, author of *Out of Africa*. "When I couldn't sleep I'd touch the globe, trace the contours of the continents in the dark," he wrote in his autobiography, *Dispatches from the Edge*. "Some nights my small fingers would hike the ridges of Everest, or struggle to reach the summit of Kilimanjaro. Many times, I rounded the Horn of Africa, more than once my ship foundering on rocks off the Cape of Good Hope. The globe was covered with names of nations that no longer exist: Tanganyika, Siam, the Belgian Congo, Ceylon. I dreamed of traveling to them all."

Death in the Family

Cooper's comfortable childhood was shattered in January 1978, when his father died while undergoing heart bypass surgery. The shock of this sudden loss triggered major changes in Cooper's emotional make-up.

"For years, I tried to swaddle the pain, encase the feelings," he admitted in his autobiography. "I boxed them up along with my father's papers, stored them away, promising one day to sort them all out. All I managed to do was deaden myself to them, detach myself from life. That works for only so long."

The death of their father also opened an emotional divide between Cooper and his brother. "After the funeral, both of us retreated into separate parts of ourselves, and I don't think we ever truly reached out to each other again," he later acknowledged.

After his father's death, Cooper became even more determined to find his own path. At age 11 he worked briefly as a model, and as a teenager he spent several of his summer vacations waiting tables at a New York City restaurant. These jobs gave him a feeling of independence and illustrated his growing resolve to succeed in life without depending on his family's wealth or influence.

EDUCATION

Cooper attended private schools in Manhattan during his childhood, including an arts-oriented high school called the Dalton School. During his years at Dalton, he signed up for a number of survival courses during summer breaks, ranging from sea kayaking excursions in Mexico to mountaineering expeditions in the Rockies. "I needed to prove to myself that I could survive on my own," he later explained.

After graduating from Dalton one semester early in 1985, Cooper organized a solo trip for himself through portions of southern and central Africa. He spent several months in Africa, traveling on foot or by truck or bus before returning home. "I knew it was in his nature to take risks, live on the edge," his mother said. "He got malaria and was in a hospital in Kenya, and he never told me about this until he came home safe."

After returning to the United States, Cooper enrolled at Yale University in New Haven, Connecticut, where he studied political science. He also served as the coxswain on the university's crew team. In crew, teams of rowers work together, while the coxswain instructs the rowers and steers the boat during competitions. But on July 22, 1988, as Cooper was preparing for his senior year at Yale, his brother Carter committed suicide by jumping from the balcony of the family's apartment in front of their mother's horrified eyes.

Television, magazine, and newspaper reporters swarmed around the family for the next few weeks, drawn by Gloria Vanderbilt's fame and wealth.

Cooper in his yearbook photo from Yale University.

Cooper was disgusted by the callous behavior of many of these journalists. "It certainly makes me more sensitive now about how I cover tragedies," he asserted. "I've never asked somebody how they feel after they've lost a member of their family. I would never use that word. How do you feel? You see that a lot on TV. It's a terrible question. The response is, 'How do you think I feel?'"

When Cooper returned to the Yale campus a few weeks later, he went to classes in a kind of daze. "I spent most of my time trying to understand what had happened," he said in *Dispatches from the Edge*. "Many times that year, I wished I had a mark, a scar, a missing limb, something children could have pointed at, at which adults could tell them not to stare. At least then they would have seen, would have known. I wouldn't have been expected to smile and mingle, meet and greet."

Cooper graduated from Yale in 1989 with a bachelor's degree. A year later, he continued his education, but under unusual circumstances. He took several months of Vietnamese language lessons at the University of Hanoi in Vietnam. But by that time, he was already making his first early forays into the world of television journalism.

CAREER HIGHLIGHTS

After leaving Yale, Cooper applied for an entry-level job at ABC News. He refused to use his family connections to launch his career, though, so he failed to even land an interview at ABC. He finally got a job as a fact-checker at Channel One, a company that broadcasts a 12-minute daily news program to thousands of high schools throughout the United States. After several months at Channel One, according to Cooper, "I came up with a plan to become a foreign correspondent. It was very simple, and monumentally stupid. I figured if I went places that were dangerous or exotic, I wouldn't have much competition, and if my stories were interesting and inexpensive, Channel One might broadcast them."

Armed with a video camera and a forged press pass, Cooper left the United States in 1991 for the Southeast Asian nation of Burma (now known as

Myanmar). He spent several weeks covering the country's growing violence between Burma's repressive military government and pro-democracy students. After Channel One bought his Burma footage, Cooper moved on to other Southeast Asian nations, including Cambodia, Thailand, and Vietnam. He spent most of his time—nearly six months—in Hanoi, the capital of Vietnam. It was during this period that he took language classes at the University of Hanoi.

In September 1992 Cooper moved on to Somalia, a civil war-torn country that sits on the coastal edge of the Horn of Africa. His coverage of the violence in Somalia was snapped up by Channel One, and in 1993 Channel One hired him as its chief international correspondent. Over the next two years, Cooper traveled all over the globe for Channel One, visiting one troubled place after another. The list of countries that he reported from included Bosnia, Croatia, Russia, Ukraine, Georgia, Israel, Cambodia, Haiti, Indonesia, South Africa, and Rwanda.

——— " ———

"I came up with a plan to become a foreign correspondent. It was very simple, and monumentally stupid. I figured if I went places that were dangerous or exotic, I wouldn't have much competition, and if my stories were interesting and inexpensive, Channel One might broadcast them."

——— " ———

Covering Wars

In most of these places, the threat of violence was a daily fact of life. And in some of them, brutal war had shattered cities and villages alike. "Anyone who tells you they aren't scared in a war zone is a fool or a liar, and probably both," Cooper wrote in *Dispatches from the Edge*. "The more places you've been, the more you know just how easy it is to get killed. It's not like in the movies. There are no slow-motion falls, no crying out the names of your loved ones. People die, and the world keeps spinning."

Cooper initially thought that he could report from these war zones without suffering any emotional damage to himself. "I thought I could get away unscathed, unchanged," he wrote. "The truth was I hadn't gotten out at all. It's impossible to block out what you see, what you hear. Even if you stop listening, the pain gets inside, seeps through the cracks you can't close up. You can't fake your way through it. I know that now. You have to absorb it all. You owe them that. You owe it to yourself as well."

After a while, Cooper realized that the things that he had seen made it difficult for him to live a "normal" life. When he returned to the United States between assignments, he discovered that he had a great deal of difficulty adjusting to the sights and sounds of a functioning society. "Coming home meant coming down," he wrote. "I'd return home to piles of bills and an empty refrigerator. Buying groceries, I'd get lost—too many aisles, too many choices; cool mist blowing over fresh fruit; paper or plastic; cash back in return? … The more I was away, the worse it got. I'd come back and couldn't speak the language. Out there the pain was palpable; you breathed it in the air. Back here, no one talked about life and death."

> "Anyone who tells you they aren't scared in a war zone is a fool or a liar, and probably both," Cooper wrote. "The more places you've been, the more you know just how easy it is to get killed. It's not like in the movies. There are no slow-motion falls, no crying out the names of your loved ones. People die, and the world keeps spinning."

Covering the News at ABC and CNN

In 1995 Cooper left Channel One and took a job at ABC News, where he became the youngest correspondent at the network. Over the next three years he kept a very busy schedule, working as a field reporter and as co-anchor of "World News Now," an ABC late-night news program. In 1998 ABC named him a contributor to their newsmagazines "20/20" and "20/20 Downtown" in addition to his other duties. Cooper contributed a number of well-received reports over the ensuing months, but he also became unhappy with his grueling schedule and some of his assignments.

In 2000 Cooper left ABC for USA Networks, which wanted him to host and produce a new weekly documentary series. Six months later, the series was cancelled and ABC Entertainment approached him about serving as the host of "The Mole," a new reality series. Cooper accepted the offer against the advice of news industry insiders who said the job would destroy his credibility as a journalist. "The Mole" was popular in its first season, but it struggled with poor ratings in its second season.

In January 2002 Cooper left his hosting duties with "The Mole" for a position on the news staff of the cable news network CNN. Defying critics who thought that his time with "The Mole" would kill his journalism career, he

Cooper on the set of his CNN news program, "Anderson Cooper 360."

quickly became a high-profile member of the CNN news team. During 2002 Cooper served as a field reporter, weekend anchor, and substitute host on various CNN programs. In March 2003 he was named co-host of a morning news show with Paula Zahn, and six months later he was given his own nightly show, "Anderson Cooper 360." When the new program was unveiled, he explained the reasoning behind the show's name. "It's 360 degrees in terms of the scope of what we're talking about, whether it's foreign policy, political events, or pop culture things."

> "
>
> "Here, you grow up believing there's a safety net, that things can never completely fall apart," Cooper wrote. "Katrina showed us all that's not true. For all the money spent on homeland security, all the preparations that have allegedly been made, we are not ready, not even for a disaster we know is coming. We can't take care of our own."
>
> "

Cooper loved hosting the show, which blended coverage of breaking news with special feature stories. "In the past, I'd make fun of anchors, but I've learned it's actually really stimulating," he said. "It's a mental exercise that I equate to running along the edge of a sand cliff that's collapsing underneath you: It's very easy for everything to go wrong and for you to fall, but if you can keep yourself upright and moving forward, it can be exhilarating. Every night it's about learning and synthesizing, being able to formulate thought and come up with questions, all in real time. It's a challenge that I really enjoy."

Hosting a high-profile news program also gave Cooper additional opportunities to travel around the world. In January 2005, for example, he gave a series of reports from Sri Lanka, where a horrible tsunami had devastated the country. He also carried out broadcasts from Iraq, the Vatican (for the April 2005 funeral of Pope John Paul II), and Florida after Hurricane Dennis hit the state in July 2005.

Reporting on Hurricane Katrina

Cooper's most notable journalistic efforts on "Anderson Cooper 360," though, came in the late summer of 2005, when Hurricane Katrina roared into the Gulf of Mexico and devastated New Orleans and many smaller communities along the Louisiana and Mississippi coastlines. The response

Cooper returned to New Orleans one year after Hurricane Katrina to report on progress. Here, he's shown at The Musician's Village, a housing project under construction by Habitat for Humanity to house musicians and artists.

to this natural disaster from state and federal authorities was woefully slow and incompetent. Thousands of desperate residents of New Orleans and other communities were left to fend for themselves for several days under nightmarish circumstances before the first help arrived. But in the first few days after Katrina reached the mainland on August 29, most lawmakers and government officials were acting as if the rescue and recovery efforts were going well.

Cooper witnessed the death and destruction in Katrina firsthand. On September 1 his frustration and anger with the terrible governmental response to the disaster finally boiled over. That anger surfaced during a televised interview with U.S. Senator Mary L. Landrieu of Louisiana.

At the beginning of the interview, Landrieu started thanking various state and federal officials for their recovery efforts. Cooper listened for a moment, then he interrupted her to declare that "for the last four days I've been seeing dead bodies in the streets.... And to listen to politicians thanking each other and congratulating each other—you know, I've got to tell you, there are a lot of people here who are very upset, and very angry, and very frustrated."

43

Cooper's words forced Landrieu to agree that the response had been inadequate. Other journalists also began asking tougher questions about the government's performance during this period. Within a matter of days, even government officials and lawmakers were apologizing for the fumbling response to Katrina.

Cooper's coverage of Hurricane Katrina brought him a flood of viewers who had never tuned in to his program before. According to many critics, these viewers were drawn by the sense that he was one of them. "He reacted the way any of us might have—raging against government officials when help didn't come fast enough, and weeping when it all got to be too much," wrote Jonathan Van Meter in *New York*. "But it wasn't just his raw emotion that set him apart ... it was his honest humanity.... He connected to those in the hurricane's path, and to the people watching at home."

For his part, Cooper believed that Hurricane Katrina changed his perception of America forever. "Here, you grow up believing there's a safety net, that things can never completely fall apart," he wrote. "Katrina showed us all that's not true. For all the money spent on homeland security, all the preparations that have allegedly been made, we are not ready, not even for a disaster we know is coming. We can't take care of our own. The world can break apart in our own backyard, and when it does many of us will simply fall off."

Dispatches from the Edge

One month after Cooper gave his dramatic, popular reports from the Gulf Coast disaster zone, CNN announced that it was expanding "Anderson Cooper 360" to two hours and moving it to 10:00 p.m. In May 2006, CBS announced that it had added Cooper to its list of contributors to "60 Minutes," the most famous newsmagazine on television.

Also in May 2006, Cooper's long-awaited autobiography was published. *Dispatches from the Edge: A Memoir of War, Disasters, and Survival* reported his experiences as a correspondent for CNN, in covering tragedies both in the United States and around the world. But it also offered a candid look at some of the tragedies in own life, showing how all of these crises affected him. *Dispatches from the Edge* immediately jumped to the top of various bestseller lists. It also received strong reviews from critics. A reviewer for the *Saturday Evening Post* called it a compelling memoir that "serves as a refreshing reminder of the power of the written word." As a writer for *Booklist* described it, "In straightforward yet passionate prose, the author recounts his experiences not only in Louisiana and Mississippi but also in sniper-riddled Sarajevo, famine-plagued Niger, tsunami-destroyed South-

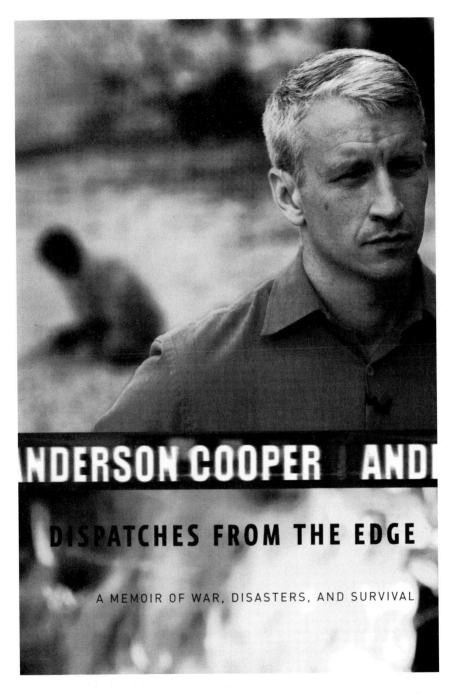

Cooper's autobiography combined his professional experience covering tragedies around the world as well as his personal experience with tragedy.

east Asia, and civil-war-ravaged Somalia. At the same time, Cooper takes a look inward, at his motivations in gravitating to dangerous adventures, and at his family history and his relations to his late father and brother and his famous mother.... He scrutinizes how those relations helped formulate his life view and compelled him to follow his dreams and desires. Cooper is both respected and popular; expect the same attitude toward his book."

Throughout 2007, Cooper traveled around the world for *Planet in Peril*, which he co-hosted with chief medical correspondent Dr. Sanjay Gupta and Animal Planet host Jeff Corwin. This four-hour documentary explored issues that threaten the planet and its inhabitants. It featured places around the world where environmental change has created environmental crises, exploring such topics as global warming, species loss, habitat loss, and overpopulation. After the documentary, Cooper continued with its theme, incorporating segments devoted to environmental issues into "Anderson Cooper 360." These segments culminated in a new program in fall 2008 called *Planet in Peril: Battle Lines*, co-hosted by Cooper, Gupta, and National Geographic host Lisa Ling. (For more information on Ling, see *Biography Today*, Apr. 2008).

> "*I love what I'm doing,*" Cooper said. "*CNN is a cool place to work because I'm able to anchor and still do a lot of field reporting. But I've never hung anything on the walls in the offices I've had because nothing seems to last very long in TV. Who knows what will happen down the road?*"

In 2007, Cooper also moderated the presidential debates sponsored by CNN and YouTube. For the Democratic debate, the presidential candidates spoke at The Citadel in Charleston, South Carolina; for the Republican debate, the presidential candidates spoke in St. Petersburg, Florida.

Cooper's autobiography, combined with his continued work as a TV reporter and anchor, has made him one of CNN's best-known journalists. He appreciates the role that he has been able to carve out with the network. "I love what I'm doing," he said. "CNN is a cool place to work because I'm able to anchor and still do a lot of field reporting. But I've never hung anything on the walls in the offices I've had because nothing seems to last very long in TV. Who knows what will happen down the road?"

HOME AND FAMILY

Cooper is single and lives in a loft in downtown Manhattan. He routinely turns aside questions about his personal life. "I understand why people might be interested," he admitted. "But I just don't talk about my personal life. The whole thing about being a reporter is that you're supposed to be an observer and to be able to adapt with any group you're in, and I don't want to do anything that threatens that."

HOBBIES AND OTHER INTERESTS

Cooper admits that he still relaxes by watching quite a bit of television. He relies on TiVo to keep up with "jaw-dropping and mind-numbing" programs like MTV's "My Super Sweet 16" and "Tiara Girls."

SELECTED WRITINGS

Dispatches from the Edge: A Memoir of War, Disasters, and Survival, 2006

HONORS AND AWARDS

Silver Plaque (Chicago International Film Festival): for reporting from Sarajevo on the Bosnian civil war
Bronze Award (National Educational Film and Video Festival): for report on political Islam
GLAAD (Gay and Lesbian Alliance Against Defamation) Media Award for Outstanding Journalism: 1999
Emmy Award: 2006 (two), to "Anderson Cooper 360" for "outstanding live coverage of a breaking news event" and "outstanding feature story"

FURTHER READING

Books

Cooper, Anderson. *Dispatches from the Edge: A Memoir of War, Disasters, and Survival,* 2006

Periodicals

Booklist, June 1, 2006, p.4
Boston Globe, Sep. 8, 2003, p.B5
Current Biography Yearbook, 2006
Entertainment Weekly, June 2, 2006, p.26
Interview, Oct. 2004, p.122
Maclean's, June 5, 2006
New York, Sep. 19, 2005

New York Times, Feb. 11, 1996, sec. 2, p.32; Sep. 12, 2005, p.E6
Newsweek, Dec. 26, 2005, p.22
O, The Oprah Magazine, July 2005, p.130
People, May 6, 1996, p.54; Jan. 15, 2001, p.77; Dec. 2, 2002, p.102
Saturday Evening Post, Sep.-Oct. 2006, p.24
Time, June 19, 2006, p.19
USA Today, June 4, 1993, p.D3
Variety, Jan. 9, 2006, p.24

Online Articles

http://www.cbsnews.com
   (*CBS News Online,* "Anderson Cooper: Coping with Grief," May 25, 2006
http://www.salon.com
   (*Salon.com,* "Method Anchor," Aug. 23, 2006)

ADDRESS

Anderson Cooper
"Anderson Cooper 360"
One CNN Center
Atlanta, GA 30303

WORLD WIDE WEB SITES

http://www.cnn.com/CNN/Programs/anderson.cooper.360

Selena Gomez 1992-

American Actor
Star of the Hit TV Show "Wizards of Waverly Place"

BIRTH

Selena Gomez was born on July 22, 1992, in Grand Prairie, Texas, a suburban city located between Dallas and Fort Worth. Gomez was born when her mother, Mandy Teefy, was 16 years old. Her young parents did not stay together, and she was raised by her mother. She has no brothers or sisters. Her father is of Mexican descent, and she was named after his favorite performer, the popular Tejano singer Selena.

YOUTH

Growing up in Grand Prairie, Gomez enjoyed spending time with her friends, hanging out at the lake near her home, and going to the mall, skate parks, or the movies. One of her favorite things to do was to go on long walks around the neighborhood with her friends. Gomez recalled, "I used to walk barefoot around my neighborhood without worrying about anything. It's nice and peaceful. We could walk in the middle of the street, and there would be no cars coming at all."

Although Gomez had a large group of friends, her Mexican heritage often made her feel left out. She remembered, "I wanted to be just like my friends. I hung out with girls who had blue eyes and blonde hair and I thought, 'I want to look like them!'" Once she started acting, however, Gomez realized that her Mexican heritage set her apart in a good way. "When I went on auditions, I'd be in a room with a lot of blonde girls, and I always stood out. It actually helped that I looked different. It got me to where I am today!"

> "I wanted to be just like my friends. I hung out with girls who had blue eyes and blonde hair and I thought, 'I want to look like them!'" But when Gomez started acting, she realized that her Mexican heritage set her apart in a good way. "When I went on auditions, I'd be in a room with a lot of blonde girls, and I always stood out. It actually helped that I looked different. It got me to where I am today!"

EDUCATION

Gomez initially attended elementary school in Grand Prairie, but soon began homeschooling. After moving to Los Angeles in 2006, she studied with a tutor, usually together with the other young actors on the set of her current television show or movie.

CAREER HIGHLIGHTS

Starting Out

Gomez knew from a very young age that she wanted to become an actor. Her mother had some experience acting with local theaters in Dallas, and Gomez decided when she was six years old that she wanted to try acting too. On her seventh birthday, Gomez joined 1,400 other hopeful young ac-

Gomez appeared on "Barney & Friends" when she was only seven years old.

tors in an audition for the PBS children's television show "Barney & Friends." She won the role of Gianna, one of the children who sang and danced with Barney the purple dinosaur. Because the show was filmed about 20 minutes from Gomez's home, she was able to continue living at home and going to school as usual. She was featured in many episodes during the two years she appeared on "Barney."

This early experience helped to prepare Gomez for her acting career. As she later recalled, "I learned everything from 'Barney.' Stage directions, camera angles.... I even learned good manners." After "Barney & Friends," Gomez went on to play small roles in the 2003 movie *Spy Kids 3-D: Game Over* and the 2005 television movie *Walker, Texas Ranger: Trial by Fire.*

The Disney Channel

In 2004, when she was 12 years old, Gomez auditioned at an open casting call for The Disney Channel in Austin, Texas. She did so well at that audition that, two weeks later, she and her mother were asked to travel to Hollywood for more auditions. Disney wanted Gomez to try out for the lead role in a new TV series called "Stevie Sanchez," a spinoff of the popular "Lizzie McGuire" series. She recalls being very nervous about auditioning in Hollywood. "It was definitely scary. I was in this room full of executives and I was testing against girls who have done movies." She got the part, but Disney later decided not to produce the series.

When plans for the Disney series fell through, Gomez decided to audition for roles with other studios. She auditioned for parts in a television series and a movie to be produced by Nickelodeon. Although she had no contract with Disney at that point, she already felt some loyalty to The Disney Channel for giving her so many opportunities. She described her Nickelodeon auditions as "uncomfortable, like I was cheating on Disney." Gomez decided to wait and see if Disney had any parts for her.

> "
>
> *"I learned everything from 'Barney,'" Gomez later recalled. "Stage directions, camera angles.... I even learned good manners."*
>
> "

Her loyalty paid off, and Disney soon offered Gomez roles in two TV series pilots, "House Broken" and "The Amazing O'Malleys." She was cast in both shows, although Disney planned to produce only one of the two shows for the 2006 TV season. She and her mother moved from Texas to Los Angeles to prepare for filming to begin. "It was hard," Gomez admitted. "It was almost a test of how badly I really wanted to pursue acting....It was really tough to leave my friends behind." Then Disney decided not to make either of the shows after all. But she wasn't out of work for long. Disney gave her a guest role in a 2006 episode of the hit show "The Suite Life of Zack and Cody."

Then in 2007, on her 15th birthday, Gomez filmed a guest role on "Hannah Montana," Disney's most popular TV show. She played the recurring character of Mikayla, Hannah Montana's rival, a part that allowed her to do her own singing. This set off a flurry of publicity and attention, as fans hotly debated the relative talent and merits of Hannah Montana star Miley Cyrus versus newcomer Gomez. Gomez's success quickly led Disney to cast her in a starring role on a new TV series, "Wizards of Waverly Place."

"Wizards of Waverly Place"

"Wizards of Waverly Place" premiered on The Disney Channel in 2007. The story focuses on the adventures of a New York City family of wizards who live a double life as they try to keep their magical powers a secret. The three Russo siblings get magic lessons from their wizard father, who teaches them spells and charms in a magical laboratory hidden behind a secret door in the family's sandwich shop. As the stories unfold, viewers find that such typical teenage issues as sibling rivalry, competition with schoolmates, schoolwork, dating, and popularity are all made more complicated with the addition of magic.

Gomez plays Alex Russo, the tomboy middle sister who is always getting herself into trouble with magic. Alex and her two brothers (played by David Henrie and Jake T. Austin) often work together to get each other into—and out of—sticky situations. The three are not allowed to use magic when their parents are not around, and they quickly learn the consequences of bending that rule. In one episode, Alex magically duplicates herself so that she can be in two places at once, only to find it difficult to control both versions of herself. In another episode, she tries to sneak into a theater to see an R-rated movie, but only succeeds in getting herself trapped in the movie itself.

Although she has enjoyed playing the role of a young wizard, Gomez revealed that before "Wizards of Waverly Place," she was not particularly drawn to other popular magical characters. "I've never actually gotten into Harry Potter, but I love the special effects of the movies. They are so cool and I love magic. All of my friends are into it....I'm happy that I'm working on a magic show."

One of the things Gomez has enjoyed the most about playing Alex is her TV family, especially her two television brothers. "My mom laughs at me all the time because we're constantly in touch with one another off the set, we're always calling.... I don't have any real-life siblings so this way I can have brothers."

One of the things Gomez has enjoyed the most about playing Alex is her TV family. She has forged close relationships with the actors who play her two television brothers. She counts her costars among her closest friends, explaining, "My mom laughs at me all the time because we're constantly in touch with one another off the set, we're always calling....I don't have any real-life siblings so this way I can have brothers." The wizarding Russos are also a bicultural family, with a Mexican-American mother and an Italian-American father. This reflection of Gomez's real life family has been a bonus. "I don't know if I would've had the opportunity to be on 'Wizards of Waverly Place' if it weren't for my heritage."

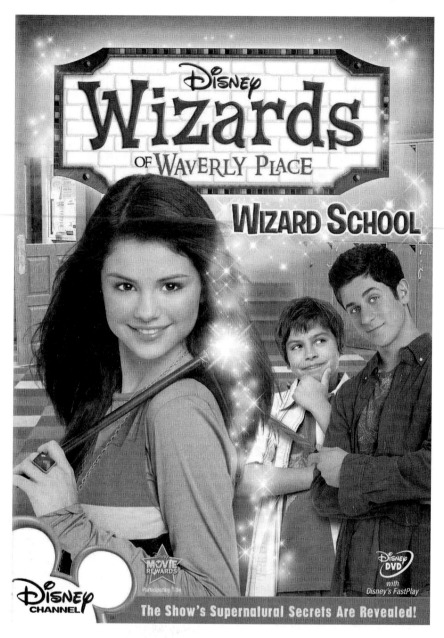

"Wizards of Waverly Place" is Gomez's first big TV series.

Gomez's favorite scenes to film are those that include the whole Russo family. "Whether it's a funny or dramatic scene, whether we're trying to solve a problem or doing magic or turning my brother invisible, it comes off best when we're with the whole family.... I think when we're all together, the show is at its strongest point. And I love being with the entire cast in a scene."

"Wizards of Waverly Place" became an instant hit with TV critics and viewers alike. Critics praised the show for its portrayal of family relationships and called the silly jokes and visual comedy entertaining for all ages. Gomez has her own explanation for the show's popularity: "The reason why it's so successful, and especially for young kids, is because kids wish they could be invisible and kids wish they could rewind time. And we bring that on screen. I know I wished that when I was younger."

—————— " ——————

Gomez enjoys singing and would like to record more music. "I think you can be more of yourself when you're singing," she explained. "You can have a little bit more control over it. It's a different process, with going into the studio and not having to worry about what you look like on camera."

—————— " ——————

Movies and Music

Along with starring in a hit TV show, Gomez has expanded her performing credits to include movies. For the 2008 animated film *Horton Hears a Who*, she provided the voices for Helga and many of the other 95 daughters of the Mayor of Whoville. "I had to change up my voice to do higher voices, and then bring it down to do lower voices. All of the Mayor's daughters look different, so I play many different characters." She appeared in the 2008 musical romantic comedy *Another Cinderella Story*, a modern retelling of the classic fairy tale co-starring Drew Seeley. He played Joey Parker, a wealthy teen who is a senior at Beverly Hills High. She played Mary Santiago, a poor girl who is forced to work for her evil guardian. The movie includes many singing and dancing numbers, which allowed the co-stars to show their talents.

Also in 2008, Gomez appeared in *Princess Protection Program*, a Disney Channel original TV movie. Princess Rosaline (played by Demi Lovato) is threatened by an evil dictator, so the Princess Protection Program, a secret agency, steps in to save her. Mason, an agent with the program, hides the princess in his own home. His daughter, Carter (played by Gomez), helps

In the animated movie Horton Hears a Who, *Gomez provided the voices for many of the Mayor's daughters, including these two getting ready for school.*

Rosie (as the princess is called) learn how to act like an ordinary girl, and Rosie helps Carter feel more confident-and more like a princess herself.

Gomez has also expanded her repertoire to include music. She performed the "Wizards of Waverly Place" theme song "Everything Is Not What It Seems." She also recorded the "Cruella De Vil" song for the *101 Dalmatians: Platinum Edition* DVD release. Disney produced a music video for the song, which has been playing regularly on The Disney Channel. In addition, she can be heard on the soundtrack for *Another Cinderella Story,* which includes several tracks by Gomez as well as duets with Seeley. Gomez enjoys singing and would like to record more music. "I think you can be more of yourself when you're singing," she explained. "You can have a little bit more control over it. It's a different process, with going into the studio and not having to worry about what you look like on camera."

HOME AND FAMILY

Gomez lives in Los Angeles, California, with her mother, her stepfather Brian, and her four dogs.

HOBBIES AND OTHER INTERESTS

Although Gomez became a Disney star almost overnight, she describes her life as normal. She does chores at home, including taking care of her own laundry, washing dishes, and cleaning her room. She enjoys surfing, cooking, photography, singing karaoke, and going to the movies. She likes to play basketball and watch basketball games, and her favorite team is the San Antonio Spurs. One of her most prized possessions is her large collection of Converse sneakers, which she wears as often as she can.

SELECTED CREDITS

"Barney & Friends," 1999-2000 (TV series)
"Wizards of Waverly Place," 2007- (TV series)
Horton Hears a Who!, 2008 (movie)
Another Cinderella Story, 2008 (movie)
Princess Protection Program, 2008 (movie)

FURTHER READING

Periodicals

Entertainment Weekly, July 20, 2007, p.46
Girls' Life, Feb./Mar. 2008, p.40
Twist Magazine, Mar. 2008, p.11, p.23, p.36, p.67
Variety, Oct. 4, 2007, p.A46
Washington Post, Oct. 19, 2007, p.C7

Online Articles

http://www.discoverygirls.com/node/414
   (Discovery Girls, "Selena Gomez's Star Power," undated)
http://www.discoverygirls.com/node/455
   (Discovery Girls, "Selena Gomez Talks to DG," Oct. 12, 2007)
http://pbskids.org/itsmylife/celebs/interviews/selena.html
   (PBSkids.org, "It's My Life: Selena Gomez," undated)
http://www.teenmag.com
   (TeenMag.com, "Getting to Know: Selena Gomez," undated)
http://www.timeforkids.com
   (Time for Kids, "10 Questions for Selena Gomez," archived story, Oct. 15, 2007)

ADDRESS

Selena Gomez
Disney Channel
Attn: Fan Mail Dept.
3800 West Alameda Avenue
Burbank, CA 91505

WORLD WIDE WEB SITE

http://tv.disney.go.com/disneychannel/wizardsofwaverlyplace

Al Gore 1948-

American Political Leader and Environmental Activist
Former Vice President of the United States, Author of
An Inconvenient Truth, and Winner of the 2007 Nobel
Peace Prize

BIRTH

Albert Arnold Gore Jr. was born on March 31, 1948, in Washington, DC. His father, Albert Arnold Gore Sr., was a former member of the U.S. Congress from Tennessee who served 14 years in the House of Representatives and 18 years in the Senate. His mother, Pauline (LaFon) Gore, was the first woman to graduate from Vanderbilt University Law School in

Tennessee. She worked as an attorney before giving up her practice to support her husband's political career. Gore's only sibling was his older sister, Nancy, who died in 1984.

YOUTH

Gore spent his first few years in Tennessee. But after that, he divided his time between two very different worlds: Washington DC, and Carthage, Tennessee. He lived part of each year with his parents and sister at the Fairfax Hotel in Washington DC. The Fairfax was an exclusive residential hotel on Embassy Row, where many of the foreign embassies are located. But at that point his family wasn't wealthy—they lived there because it was owned by a relative. His parents were very frugal, although they did pay for private education. When Gore was in Washington, he was surrounded by adults in the politically charged atmosphere of the U.S. capitol, and he was exposed there to his parents' passion for politics. But there wasn't much for a boy to do, living in a hotel.

—— " ——

"Even though I spent more time each year in Washington, Tennessee was home," Gore later recalled. "Now I'm sure that part of that was me, as a kid, absorbing my parents' insistence on the political reality of their lives, that they were representing Tennessee in Washington. I'm sure I picked up a lot of that as a child. But it was more than that." For Gore, Tennessee was where "the human relationships were much warmer."

—— " ——

Gore spent the remainder of his time on his family's farm in Carthage, Tennessee. In Tennessee, he was often left in the care of the Thompson family, who were tenant farmers. According to the *New York Times,* "[Gore] lived in two worlds that could hardly have been more different.... [He] essentially adopted the Thompsons as a second family. . . Their home became a kind of emotional citadel, a refuge from the larger world, where great expectations awaited him." There he swam in the Caney Fork River and worked alongside the hired. The natural, casual environment of his time on the farm stood in sharp contrast to the setting of wealth and power he experienced in Washington.

"Even though I spent more time each year in Washington, Tennessee was home," Gore later recalled. "Now I'm sure that part of that was me, as a kid, absorbing my parents' insistence on the political reality of their lives, that they were representing Tennessee in Washington. I'm sure I picked up a lot of that as a child. But it was more than that." For Gore, Tennessee was where he had close friends and where "the human relationships were much warmer."

But life in Tennessee wasn't all fun and games. Gore's father was determined that Al would develop a strong work ethic, and he'd wake his son at 6:00 a.m. to join the workers in the field. The younger Gore would bale hay, cut tobacco, clear fields, clean the hogs' pens, or whatever the farm hands were doing. In fact, his father usually assigned the worst tasks to his son.

The Gores were a family of high achievers, and expectations were especially high for young Al. His father was strict and taught Gore from an early age to work hard in preparation for a bright future. As a Congress member's son, he was encouraged to pursue a career in politics. Being somewhat in the public eye because of his father's position in Congress, Gore developed an early sense of reserve and caution that made him seem more adult than his peers.

EDUCATION

In Washington DC, Gore attended St. Alban's Episcopal School for Boys, a highly competitive and elite private school modeled after British schools. He was an honor student and captain of the football team. In his high school yearbook, Gore was called the model of the all-American young man.

Gore entered Harvard University in 1965. In addition to his studies, he was president of the freshman council and worked as a messenger for the *New York Times*, where he ran errands in the newspaper's offices. During his last summer before graduation, he was the chairman of Tennessee Youth for McCarthy, an organization working on Eugene McCarthy's 1968 presidential campaign. Gore graduated from Harvard *cum laude* (with distinction) in 1969, earning a bachelor's degree in government.

FIRST JOBS

After graduating from Harvard, Gore found himself in a painful and confusing situation. The Vietnam War was in full swing, thousands of young men were being drafted into military service, and war protestors were holding demonstrations all across the country. Meanwhile, Gore's father was in a tight race for re-election to the Senate. As an outspoken critic of U.S. military involvement in Vietnam, the senior Gore was being called unfit to rep-

From 1969 to 1971, during the Vietnam War, Gore served in the U.S. Army; he was assigned to be a reporter and was stationed in Vietnam.

resent the people of Tennessee. Considering all of this, his son realized that he had an important decision to make about what he would do next.

Like many other young men of his generation, Gore opposed the war in Vietnam and seriously considered resisting the draft. But he chose to volunteer for enlistment in the U.S. Army so that his actions would not reflect poorly on his father. Gore's family did not pressure him to enlist—they urged him to follow his conscience, and his mother even offered to flee with him to Canada if he decided to avoid military service. Gore made his decision to enlist both as a point of personal honor and as a political sacrifice. From 1969 to 1971, he served in the U.S. Army in Vietnam, working as a reporter with the 20th Engineering Battalion outside Saigon.

Serving as an army reporter in Vietnam led Gore to a career in journalism when he returned to the U.S. From 1971 to 1976, he worked for the *Tennessean* in Nashville, first as a reporter and later as an editorial writer. During the same time, he also enrolled in the School of Religion at Vanderbilt University. He decided to attend divinity school, he said, not to become a minister but instead "to study the spiritual issues that were most important to me at the time … to find some answers." Gore transferred to Vanderbilt's law school in 1974. He planned to use the degree

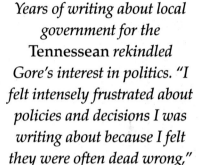

Years of writing about local government for the Tennessean *rekindled Gore's interest in politics. "I felt intensely frustrated about policies and decisions I was writing about because I felt they were often dead wrong," he recalled. "But as a journalist I could do nothing to change them."*

in tandem with his already budding career in journalism. In addition to studying and working for the *Tennessean,* Gore also worked as a real estate developer and livestock and tobacco farmer. He insisted that he was not interested in a career in politics, although that soon changed.

CAREER HIGHLIGHTS

Entering Congress

In 1976, when Gore was 28 years old, he received the unexpected news that the U.S. Representative from his home district had decided to retire. Despite his earlier objections to a career in politics, Gore now found that years of writing about local government for the *Tennessean* had rekindled his interest in public service. "I felt intensely frustrated about policies and decisions I was writing about because I felt they were often dead wrong," he recalled. "But as a journalist I could do nothing to change them." Gore entered the Democratic primaries, winning his party's nomination by a narrow margin. He went on to win the general

Gore speaking with potential voters in 1976, before his election to the U.S. House of Representatives.

election, and in 1977 he moved to Washington, DC, to take his place in the U.S. House of Representatives.

In Washington, Gore quickly gained a reputation as a tough investigator and a thorough researcher—skills he had learned in his work as a reporter. He involved himself in a variety of issues, ranging from organ transplants, to housing for the poor, to the economic development of the Tennessee River and surrounding areas. During his time in the House of Representatives, Gore also began focusing on health-related environmental issues. He held the first Congressional hearing on toxic waste, bringing national attention to the damage caused by toxic waste dumping near Memphis, Tennessee and the Love Canal neighborhood near Niagara Falls, New York. He also played an important role in the passage of the "Superfund" bill in 1980, which provided money to clean up chemical spills and toxic waste dumps.

Becoming a Senator

In 1983, after serving four terms in the House of Representatives, Gore decided to run for the U.S. Senate. He ran a hard campaign and won easily, but a cloud fell over the victory. His sister Nancy, a tireless worker through the years on her brother's behalf, died of lung cancer before the 1984 election, without ever knowing that he had won.

In the Senate, Gore continued to earn his reputation as a workhorse. While he served on a number of committees with diverse interests, he was by this time mainly concerned with environmental topics and nuclear arms control. He looked for a balance, he said, between "national power and security on the one hand, and long-term human survival on the other." Gore diligently studied complex issues, talked with experts, and impressed his peers with his uncanny ability to absorb and process the most scientific details of new technologies. He was recognized as an authority in his special areas of interest.

Based on his successes in Congress, Gore declared his intent to run for president in early 1987. Many observers said that his driving ambition pushed him to seek the highest level of government. But he was unable to adequately define his policies or himself as a candidate, and he ultimately withdrew from the presidential race. He returned to his seat in the Senate and focused on furthering his work there.

Gore became the chairperson of the Senate Subcommittee on Science, Technology, and Space. In this position, he focused on issues related to

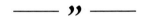

Gore's work as a legislator helped pave the way for the development of the Internet. According to former Republican House Speaker Newt Gingrich. "Gore is the person who, in the Congress, most systematically worked to make sure that we got to an Internet."

space exploration, environmental protection, and linking the nation via supercomputers—a project that would prove to be the foundation of the Internet and World Wide Web. In the 1970s, the Internet was a closed system that was limited to the Pentagon and a few universities. It was mainly used for research by scientists. In the late 1980s, Gore sponsored two bills that turned the fledgling computer network into a true "information superhighway," a term he popularized to describe the proposed new system that would be accessible to everyone. According to former Republican House Speaker Newt Gingrich. "Gore is the person who, in the Congress, most systematically worked to make sure that we got to an Internet."

Tragedy Strikes

By 1989, Gore was married with four children. That year, the family suffered a tragic accident. Gore's son Albert III, then six years old, had darted in front of a car and was thrown 30 feet into the air and dragged across the

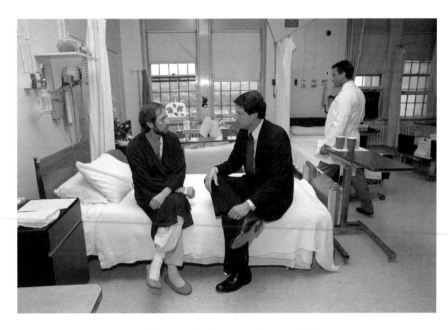

*While running for president in 1987,
Gore visited with this AIDS patient in Los Angeles.*

pavement before his horror-stricken father's eyes. He lay in the gutter, re-called Gore, with his eyes open in an "empty stare of death." After exten-sive surgery, a lengthy hospital stay, and a long period of recuperation, the boy eventually made a full recovery. Gore has said that the traumatic acci-dent that almost took his son's life led him to "confront some difficult and painful questions about what I am really seeking in my own life, and why."

Earth in the Balance

While his son recovered from the accident, Gore realized that he wanted to "reevaluate serious issues." He wondered if he had done enough to en-sure his children's future. He saw a connection between "the global envi-ronmental crisis and [his own] inner crisis that is, for lack of a better word, spiritual." Gore began to consider the effect an environmentally unstable world would have on his four children.

Gore began writing his book *Earth in the Balance: Ecology and the Human Spirit* during his son's 1989 hospital stay. The book is divided into two main sections. The first section includes a complete explanation of the worldwide environmental crisis, covering issues such as global warming, acid rain, deforestation, and overpopulation. The second section provides a series of recommended steps to fix the problems, such as the creation of an international environmental council to monitor activities that damage the environment.

The book attracted a lot of attention from the media and critics because it discussed complicated environmental issues and solutions in terms that everyone could understand. Some people criticized Gore's ideas as "unworkable" and said that his proposed solutions would result in too much harm to the U.S. economy. The book received the harshest criticism from members of the Republican Party, which published a statement that said, "*Earth in the Balance* is plagued by a combination of liberalism, elitism, hypocrisy, and hyperbole, punctuated by an unhealthy extremism." Meanwhile, environmental activists praised Gore for presenting complex scientific issues in language that was easy to understand. A reviewer writing in *Business Week* called the book "a useful primer on the world's environmental problems." The *New York Times Book Review* said that Gore's writing was "fresh and compelling." And *Time* praised Gore as an "intellectual politician who is more committed to important issues than most of his colleagues."

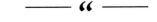

In reviewing Earth in the Balance, *Gore's first book on environmental issues,* Time *magazine praised him as an "intellectual politician who is more committed to important issues than most of his colleagues."*

Although Gore had been working on environmental issues for many years already, the 1992 publication of *Earth in the Balance* gave him a public reputation as an environmental pioneer. In that same year, he served as an official U.S. representative to the Earth Summit held in Rio de Janeiro, Brazil. The Earth Summit was a conference held by the United Nations to focus on global environmental issues. The largest environmental conference held up to that time, it was attended by representatives of the governments of more than 170 nations.

Becoming Vice President

Gore was offered another major opportunity in 1992—the chance to become Vice President of the United States. When Bill Clinton secured the Democratic Party's nomination in the presidential elections that year, he asked Gore to be his running mate. Balancing one another's strengths and

As vice president, Gore met in the Oval Office with President Bill Clinton and Chief of Staff Erskine Bowles.

weaknesses, the two men pooled their considerable resources for a campaign that ultimately lead to victory.

Clinton was an expert on domestic and economic issues, and Gore was knowledgeable about foreign affairs. The president-elect had avoided the draft, but his running mate was a Vietnam veteran. Clinton's experience was limited to state administration, while Gore knew his way around the nation's capital. Clinton had been publicly accused of infidelity, while the Gore marriage stood up to scrutiny. The governor of Arkansas was an exuberant man of the people, but the senator from Tennessee was less comfortable in public.

In November 1992, the Clinton-Gore ticket beat their Republican opponents, President George H.W. Bush and Vice President Dan Quayle. Gore was inaugurated as the 45th Vice President of the United States on January 20, 1993. President Clinton and Vice President Gore were re-elected to a second term in 1996, and Gore was sworn in again on January 20, 1997.

During his two terms as vice president (1993-2001), Gore served as an advisor to President Clinton and as the President of the U.S. Senate, a member of the National Security Council, and the head of a wide range of Administration initiatives. Because of his close relationship with President

Clinton, and his involvement in so many critical issues of the time, Gore has been called one of the most influential vice presidents in U.S. history.

As vice president, Gore continued to focus attention on environmental issues on a worldwide scale. He worked tirelessly to raise awareness of the growing environmental problems caused by such human factors as automobile exhaust and toxic waste. In December 1997, against the objections of many top U.S. government officials, Gore attended an international environmental issues meeting in Kyoto, Japan. The goal of the meeting was to create the Kyoto Accords—a worldwide strategy to reduce global warming. The governments of European countries wanted the U.S. government to reduce the amount of air pollution produced by Americans. Although the U.S. government ultimately did not sign the Kyoto Accords, Gore's presence and diplomatic negotiation ensured that nearly all of the other attending governments signed on to reduce the amount of air pollution they produced.

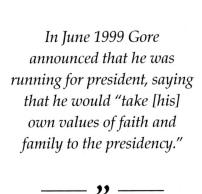

In June 1999 Gore announced that he was running for president, saying that he would "take [his] own values of faith and family to the presidency."

Running for President

With President Clinton's second term in office coming to a close, Gore decided that he would run for president himself in the 2000 election. He announced his candidacy in June 1999, saying that he would "take [his] own values of faith and family to the presidency." In August 2000, Gore won the Democratic Party's nomination for president. He campaigned against George W. Bush, the son of the previous president, George H.W. Bush.

The race between Gore and George W. Bush was close from the very beginning of the campaign. In polls conducted during the summer of 2000, the two candidates were separated by only 10% of potential voters. In such a heated contest, not even the three televised debates between Gore and Bush could produce a clear winner. During the debates, the candidates answered questions about their ideas for education, foreign policy, and other important issues. Opinion polls conducted after the debates showed that voters were still almost evenly divided between Gore and Bush.

Indeed, the 2000 presidential election proved to be one of the closest—and strangest—elections in U.S. history. After the voting took place on

November 7, and after most of the votes were counted, it became clear that the outcome of the election would depend entirely on the votes of the state of Florida. A great controversy then developed over the manner in which Florida votes had been collected and counted. There were accusations that ballots were misleading, causing people to vote for a different candidate than the one they intended. More accusations claimed that ballots were tampered with or even thrown away without being counted. Inconsistent election rules also seemed to have prevented many people from voting at all.

In the midst of all the confusion and suspicion, a preliminary total of Florida votes indicated that Gore had slightly more votes than Bush, although less than one half of one percent of votes separated the two candidates. It was an extremely close result—so close, in fact, that a mandatory automatic recount of votes was required by law.

Counting the Votes

The first recount of votes was done by machine. The machine recount revealed further problems with the punch-card ballots used by some Florida voting precincts. Many ballots were rejected—and therefore not counted—by the machines. After the recount by machine, Bush emerged slightly ahead of Gore. But due to the large number of rejected ballots, Gore and the Democratic Party demanded a second recount to be done by hand.

An investigation into the accusations of ballot-tampering and the problems with rejected ballots revealed that many of the punch-card ballots were torn. Tiny slips of paper, called chads, were supposed to be punched out from the ballot to indicate which candidate received a vote. The problem was that some of the chads were not fully detached from the ballot, and were hanging by one or two corners, while other chads were only indented and not punched out at all. The inconsistent punches and torn slips of paper were what had caused so many problems with the vote counting machines.

The torn ballots caused even more problems during the hand recount. A heated argument developed between voting officials and officials from the Republican and Democratic Parties about how to interpret the torn ballots. The outcome of the election depended entirely upon how the voter's intention was interpreted, based on the appearance of the hanging or indented chad. Using one interpretation, Bush would win by more than 1,700 votes. But using another interpretation, Gore would win by fewer than 200 votes. The debate raged on for weeks, as Americans waited to learn who the new president would be.

Gore at a rally during the 2000 presidential campaign, flanked by his wife, Tipper Gore, and President Bill Clinton.

The recount by hand proved to be the most controversial issue. When the results of a partial hand recount indicated that Bush would be the winner, Gore and the Democrats challenged the decision in court. The case went all the way to the U.S. Supreme Court, which eventually issued a historic 5-to-4 ruling (in itself a very close decision) that any further recounting would be unconstitutional. When this decision was made, Bush was ahead by slightly more than 500 votes—a very small number considering the overall total number of votes.

All of the confusion had been focused on Florida's popular vote—the votes cast by the citizens of Florida. U.S. Presidential elections are determined by the votes of the Electoral College, whose votes are generally given to the candidate who receives the most popular votes in a particular state. In order to win a presidential election, a candidate must have a minimum of 270 of the total 538 available electoral votes. Because the electoral votes of most states are awarded by a strict majority, and not based on population or total number of votes cast, it is possible for a candidate to receive the most popular votes nationwide and yet not gain enough electoral votes to win the election.

And that is what happened in the 2000 election. When the Florida vote-counting crisis occurred, 99% of all the popular votes in the nation had been counted. Gore had been awarded 255 electoral votes and Bush had received 246. Although Gore had almost a half million more popular votes when the Supreme Court stopped the recounts, Florida's 25 electoral votes went to Bush, making him the winner with a total of 271 electoral votes. This was the first time since 1888 that the candidate with the most popular votes did not win the election.

Once the Supreme Court decision was made and Bush was declared the winner, Gore conceded defeat. On December 13, more than one month after the November 7 election, he said, "Let there be no doubt: While I strongly disagree with the court's decision, I accept it.... And tonight for the sake of our unity as a people and the strength of our democracy, I offer my concession." Gore emphasized the need for unity and reconciliation after the bitterness of the vote-counting crisis and called on Americans to support the new president. "We are a nation of laws and the presidential election of 2000 is over."

> "Let there be no doubt: While I strongly disagree with the court's decision, I accept it," Gore said after the Supreme Court decision that led to Bush's presidential win. "And tonight for the sake of our unity as a people and the strength of our democracy, I offer my concession." Gore emphasized the need for unity and reconciliation and called on Americans to support the new president. "We are a nation of laws and the presidential election of 2000 is over."

Leaving Politics

After suffering the devastating loss of the 2000 presidential election, and wanting to get away from any further controversy, Gore withdrew from public life. He moved to Nashville and concentrated on building a new life as a private citizen. He had served 25 years in federal government and needed to decide what to do next. Recalling the weeks just after the election, Gore said, "That was a hard blow, but what do you do? You make the best of it." He spent time with his family and went on a vacation with his wife. He accepted a visiting professorship and taught journalism classes at universities around the country. He even considered running for president again in 2004, but changed his mind after the terrorist attacks of September 11, 2001. Believing that the U.S. again needed unity, Gore used the occasion that he had planned to announce his candidacy to publicly call for Americans to support President Bush.

An Inconvenient Truth

While Gore was struggling to find a new purpose for his work, his wife Tipper suggested that he return to the issue that had been most important to him for many years—the environment. She encouraged him to put together an updated version of a slideshow he had once created to teach people about global warming. The first time he used the presentation was in 1989, when he was writing *Earth in the Balance*. Gore had carried an easel to a dinner party and stood on a chair to display a large chart that he drew, showing the rise of air pollution.

The slideshow presentation focused on the same issues that Gore had been talking about since the 1970s. He converted his old slides to a computerized presentation and began giving his lecture anywhere he could find an audience. Recalling those early lectures, Tipper Gore said to *Time*, "We were on tour, doing the slide show, and men and women would come up to Al after, silently weeping." Gore's presentation was striking a chord with many who were deeply affected by what he had to say. This was the beginning of *An Inconvenient Truth*, which would soon become an Academy Award-winning documentary film with several companion books.

The central message of *An Inconvenient Truth* is that global warming threatens all life on earth, and a solution must be found quickly in order to avoid the worst consequences. "We have become capable of doing catastrophic damage without realizing it," Gore explained. "We've quadrupled the population in less than a century, amplified the power of technology many thousands of times over, and we haven't matched those changes with a shift in our thinking that lets us take into account the long-term consequences of our actions." But in addition to raising awareness of the problem, Gore also offered hope for a realistic solution. "I believe this is the rare crisis that requires a fundamental shift in public opinion at the grass-roots level.... The path to a solution lies through changing the minds of the American people.... It is very possible to start leveling it out within the next five years.... I'm trying to say to you, be a part of the change. No one

An Inconvenient Truth *has taken many forms: it has been a lecture, a documentary film, a book for adults, and a book for young adults, as shown here.*

else is going to do it. The politicians are paralyzed. The people have to do it for themselves!"

As Gore traveled around the country to present his lecture, he spoke to a group in Hollywood, California. Afterwards, he was approached by movie producers who wanted to make a documentary film version to bring the message to more people. At first, he later said, "I was dubious that anyone would be willing to make a movie with so much science in it." Despite his doubts, the movie came together very quickly and was released in 2006. It became an unexpected success, both in theaters and in sales of the DVD version. *An Inconvenient Truth* won two Academy Awards in 2007, for Best Documentary Feature and Best Original Song. Companion books have been published for adult and young adult readers, with translations into 28 languages for worldwide distribution.

The documentary and book have received overwhelmingly positive reviews. Gore's presentation has been called "scarily persuasive" and a "case for immediate action." *Booklist* praised the young adult version of the book, saying "few, if any, books for youth offer such a dynamic look at the climate issues threatening our planet." There has been some criticism of *An Inconvenient Truth,* which has focused on the idea that Gore exaggerated the seriousness of the problem.

In spite of this criticism, *An Inconvenient Truth* helped to energize the "green" environmental movement that subsequently swept the nation. A movie critic writing for *Time* said, "Gore's film helped trigger one of the most dramatic opinion shifts in history as Americans suddenly realized they must change the way they live." The movie has inspired thousands of people to get involved in environmental activism. Gore has trained more than 1,000 volunteers from all walks of life to give his lecture and also train others to do so. The list of trained speakers includes such celebrities as actress Cameron Diaz and Philadelphia Eagles linebacker Dhani Jones. On July 7, 2007, the Live Earth global music festival, inspired by *An Inconvenient Truth,* was televised around the world, with performances on all seven continents. The festival was designed to increase awareness of and involvement in environmental causes.

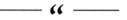

"We have become capable of doing catastrophic damage without realizing it," Gore explained. "We've quadrupled the population in less than a century, amplified the power of technology many thousands of times over, and we haven't matched those changes with a shift in our thinking that lets us take into account the long-term consequences of our actions."

The Nobel Peace Prize

In 2007, Gore was awarded the Nobel Peace Prize for his work raising public awareness of global warming and climate change. He shared the

———— **"** ————

"We, the human species, are confronting a planetary emergency—a threat to the survival of our civilization.... The future is knocking at our door right now.... [The] next generation will ask us one of two questions. Either they will ask, 'What were you thinking; why didn't you act?' Or they will ask instead: 'How did you find the moral courage to rise and successfully resolve a crisis that so many said was impossible to solve?'"

———— **"** ————

prestigious award with the Intergovernmental Panel on Climate Change, a United Nations network of scientists. In its formal citation, the Nobel committee honored Gore for his work "to build up and disseminate greater knowledge about man-made climate change." The committee also called Gore "the single individual who has done most to create greater worldwide understanding of the measures needed to be adopted."

In accepting the Peace Prize, Gore said this: "We, the human species, are confronting a planetary emergency—a threat to the survival of our civilization that is gathering ominous and destructive potential even as we gather here. But there is hopeful news as well: we have the ability to solve this crisis and avoid the worst—though not all—of its consequences, if we act boldly, decisively, and quickly.... The future is knocking at our door right now. Make no mistake, the next generation will ask us one of two questions. Either they will ask, 'What were you thinking; why didn't you act?' Or they will ask instead: 'How did you find the moral courage to rise and successfully resolve a crisis that so many said was impossible to solve?'"

MARRIAGE AND FAMILY

Al Gore has been married since May 19, 1970, to Mary Elizabeth Aitcheson, known as Tipper, a childhood nickname taken from a favorite nursery rhyme. The couple met at a high school dance and, after only a few dates, knew that they would one day marry. Tipper holds undergraduate and graduate degrees in psychology and has worked as a professional photographer. She is well known for her controversial campaign against profanity and violence in rock music and for her success in forcing record companies to attach warning labels to albums with explicit lyrics.

Gore won the 2007 Nobel Peace Prize for his environmental work. He shared the prize with the Intergovernmental Panel on Climate Change, a United Nations group of scientists represented by Rajendra Pachauri. Gore and Pachauri are shown here receiving their Nobel medals and diplomas.

The Gores have four children—Karenna, Kristin, Sarah, and Albert III—all now grown. They also have two grandchildren, Wyatt Gore Schiff and Anna Hunger Schiff.

The Gores live in Nashville, Tennessee, in a 1915 mansion that has been remodeled to be as energy efficient as possible. They also own a farm in Tennessee, located across the Caney Fork River from Gore's parents' farm. In addition, the Gores have homes in California and Virginia.

SELECTED CREDITS

Earth in the Balance: Ecology and the Human Spirit, 1992 (book)
An Inconvenient Truth, 2006 (film)
An Inconvenient Truth: The Planetary Emergency of Global Warming and What We Can Do About It, 2006 (book)
An Inconvenient Truth: The Crisis of Global Warming, 2007 (juvenile book)
The Assault on Reason, 2007 (book)

HONORS AND AWARDS

One of Ten Outstanding Young Americans (Jaycees): 1980
Humanitas Prize, Special Award: 2006, for *An Inconvenient Truth* film
Quill Award in History/Current Events/Politics: 2006, for *An Inconvenient Truth*; 2007, for *The Assault on Reason*
Academy Awards (Academy of Motion Picture Arts and Sciences): 2007 (two awards), Best Documentary Feature and Best Original Song, for *An Inconvenient Truth*
Nobel Peace Prize: 2007

FURTHER READING

Books

Hillstrom, Kevin. *People in the News: Al Gore*, 2008 (juvenile)
Jeffrey, Laura S. *Al Gore: Leader for the New Millennium*, 1999 (juvenile)
Maraniss, David. *The Prince of Tennessee: The Rise of Al Gore*, 2000
Sapet, Kerrily. *Political Profiles: Al Gore*, 2008 (juvenile)
Sergis, Diana K. *Bush v. Gore: Controversial Political Election Case, Landmark Supreme Court Cases Series*, 2003 (juvenile)
Turque, Bill. *Inventing Al Gore*, 2000

Periodicals

Current Biography Yearbook, 2001
New York Times, Oct. 13, 2007

New York Times Magazine, Oct 25, 1992, p.40; May 20, 2007, p.42
Time, Aug. 8, 2005, p.32; June 5, 2006, p.24; May 28, 2007, p.30; Dec. 31,
    2007-Jan. 7, 2008, p.98
USA Today, Apr. 25, 2007, p.D1
Vanity Fair, Oct. 2007
Washington Post, Oct. 3, 1999, p.A1; Oct. 10, 1999, p.A1; Dec. 11, 2007,
    p.A14
Wired, May 2006

Online Articles

http://www.nytimes.com/library/politics/camp/052200wh-dem-gore.html
    (New York Times, "Al Gore's Journey: A Boyhood Divided—A Boy's Life
    In and Out of the Family Script," May 22, 2000)
http://www.nytimes.com/2007/10/13/world/13nobel.html
    (New York Times, "Gore Shares Peace Prize for Climate Change Work,"
    Oct. 13, 2007)
http://www.pbs.org/wgbh/pages/frontline/shows/choice2000/gore/
    (PBS, "The Choice 2000: Al Gore," no date)
http://www.rollingstone.com/news/story/10688399/al_gore_30
    (Rolling Stone, "Al Gore 3.0," June 28, 2006)
http://www.vanityfair.com/politics/features/2007/10/gore200710
    (Vanity Fair, "Going After Gore," Oct. 2007)
http://www.washingtonpost.com/wp-srv/politics/campaigns/wh2000/stories/
    gore101099a.htm
    (Washington Post, "Al Gore: Growing Up in Two Worlds," Oct. 10, 1999)
http://www.wired.com/wired/archive/14.05/gore_pr.html
    (Wired, "The Resurrection of Al Gore," May 2006)

ADDRESS

Al Gore
2100 West End Avenue
Suite 620
Nashville, TN 37203

WORLD WIDE WEB SITES

http://www.algore.com
http://www.wecansolveit.org

Eli Manning 1981-

American Professional Football Player with the New York Giants

Most Valuable Player of the 2008 Super Bowl

BIRTH

Elisha "Eli" Nelson Manning was born on January 3, 1981, in New Orleans, Louisiana. His father, Archie Manning, was a legendary quarterback who starred in college for the University of Mississippi (known as Ole Miss), then went on to play 14 seasons in the National Football League (NFL). He spent most of his professional career, which spanned from 1971 to 1984, as the starting quarterback for the New Orleans Saints.

Archie Manning met Eli's mother, Olivia Manning, at Ole Miss, where she was homecoming queen as a senior.

Eli Manning has two older brothers, Cooper and Peyton. Cooper, who is five years older than Eli, was a star football player in high school, but a spinal injury forced him to give up the game before college. Peyton, who is two years older than Eli, enjoyed a tremendous college career with the University of Tennessee Volunteers. He then went on to become one of the top quarterbacks in the NFL.

——— " ———

Eli Manning sometimes found himself the target of unwanted attention from his older siblings. "I got pounded on a little bit," he admitted. "Cooper was two years older than Peyton, so he used to be able to pick on him a little bit. All of a sudden I come along, and I'm five years younger, and Peyton needs someone to beat on a little bit, and I took a pounding. At the time I didn't really enjoy it, but it made me tough."

——— " ———

YOUTH

Manning grew up in a family whose activities revolved around sports. His older brothers often went with their father to team practices, where they were treated as lovable mascots by Archie's massive teammates. They even got their little ankles taped once in a while by team trainers, just like their dad. These experiences instilled in both Cooper and Peyton a deep love for football. Eli, on the other hand, was only three years old when his father retired from the NFL, so he never had the opportunity to watch his dad practice or play in an actual NFL game.

As he grew older, Eli sometimes felt overshadowed by his older brothers. They were big strapping boys who loved nothing more than to play sports and quiz their father about his NFL playing days. The three of them usually dominated dinner table conversations while Eli, who was naturally shy, listened quietly. At other times, he sometimes found himself the target of unwanted attention from his older siblings. "I got pounded on a little bit," he admitted. "Cooper was two years older than Peyton, so he used to be able to pick on him a little bit. All of a sudden I come along, and I'm five years younger, and Peyton needs someone to beat on a little bit, and I took a pounding. At the time I didn't really enjoy it, but it made me tough."

Eli also toughened up in the intense backyard football games that his brothers often organized. He did the dirty work of snapping the ball and

Eli (center) with his brothers, Peyton and Cooper,
at Ole Miss, his father's alma mater.

blocking for the older boys, who did most of the passing and receiving. When Peyton grew into a highly touted high school quarterback, Eli spent hours in the yard catching passes from his rifle-armed brother. He got so many bruises on his arms from catching these hard-thrown balls that Peyton finally invented some homemade padding for him. "I got him a great big T-shirt, a triple-X T-shirt, and stuffed it full of pillows and put towels in the sleeves," recalled Peyton. "He looked like the Stay-Puft Marshmallow Man."

As the years passed by, though, Eli grew to be the same size as his brothers. He remembered one occasion when this reality hit home for Peyton. Throughout Eli's youth, he had always lost to Peyton at whatever sport they played, from football to ping pong. But this losing streak came to an end during a one-on-one basketball game when Peyton was visiting from college. "I was about 17, 18 years old," Eli recalled. "It was in the backyard.... Neither one of us has a great shot, so we'd back each other in, and you're getting fouled.... We both had cuts, and it was a brutal game." A short time later, Peyton challenged his little brother to a rematch. But their father took the backboard down first. "Dad got a little worried about one of us getting hurt or something, so that ended our basketball game," said Eli. "We haven't played since."

Eli's home environment became quieter as his brothers grew older. Cooper and Peyton spent a lot of time at sporting and other school events, and after they graduated from high school they moved on to college. During these years Eli's close relationship with his mother became even stronger. They established a routine of going out to eat at least once a week, and she took Eli with her on so many shopping trips for antiques that he developed a taste for antiques himself. "They have that special bond that you see between mamas and their baby boys," his father explained.

For his part, Eli declared that his mother was the cornerstone of the Manning household. "Growing up, we would have been lost and clueless without her," he said. "She ran the household and was our biggest supporter." Friends of the Manning family, meanwhile, praised both parents for creating a loving and supportive home environment. "They were taught to respect adults and have the right manners," said Billy Van Devender, who was best man at their wedding. "All Archie and Olivia wanted was for their kids to be normal. You don't see them flaunting their success. The whole family is warm and generous, a joy to be around."

EDUCATION

Manning had trouble learning to read in his first years at school. "As a child, it's embarrassing and frustrating," he remembered. "They call on students to read out loud in class and it's one of those deals where you're praying the whole time that they don't call on you." His mother, though, helped him get through his early struggles and develop into a top student. "She worked with me and stayed patient," Eli said. "Her laid-back attitude and her soft Southern drawl helped me keep calm about it. She's the one who kept telling me it would all work out and it did."

Like his brothers, Manning attended Isidore Newman High School in New Orleans. And like Peyton, Eli was a star quarterback on the school's football team. By the time he graduated from high school in 1999, the youngest Manning boy was being recruited by major college programs across the country. "Eli has everything Peyton had when he was here, a strong arm, good size, and excellent leadership ability," said Isidore Newman Head Coach Frank Gendusa. "He could eventually be as attractive to the pros as Peyton and Archie."

Manning eventually decided to play football for the Ole Miss Rebels, the same program that had made his father a star. In fact, Archie Manning enjoys such legendary status at the school that the campus speed limit is 18 miles per hour, in honor of his jersey number. Peyton had decided to attend the University of Tennessee in part because of the huge pressure that he would have felt to duplicate his father's career at Ole Miss. Eli agreed that going to Ole Miss would put additional pressure on him, but he decided that it was still the right school for him.

Eli Manning played football at Ole Miss, but he also excelled in the classroom throughout his years there. His name regularly appeared on various academic honor rolls, and he even won a postgraduate academic scholarship. He graduated from the University of Mississippi in December 2003 with a bachelor's degree in marketing.

> —— " ——
>
> *Manning had trouble learning to read. "As a child, it's embarrassing and frustrating. They call on students to read out loud in class and it's one of those deals where you're praying the whole time that they don't call on you," he remembered. "My mother worked with me and stayed patient. Her laid-back attitude and her soft Southern drawl helped me keep calm about it. She's the one who kept telling me it would all work out and it did."*
>
> —— " ——

CAREER HIGHLIGHTS

College-University of Mississippi Rebels

Manning made an even bigger impact on the Ole Miss football field. When he first enrolled at his father's alma mater, he admitted that he did not know whether he could be as successful as Peyton, who was already tearing up the college football world at Tennessee. "I was nervous and scared when I went to school because I didn't know if I could complete a pass in college," he admitted. "Forget about trying to be like Peyton."

Manning redshirted as a freshman (a "redshirt" is a college player who practices with the team but does not play in games so that he can preserve four years of eligibility). He did not play much the following season. But he was the starting quarterback for Ole Miss the next three seasons, and during that time he lived up to the legendary Manning name. Torching some of the best defenses in all of college football with his throwing arm, Eli guided Ole Miss to three consecutive winning seasons.

> "
>
> *The transition from high school to college football was tough for Manning. "I was nervous and scared when I went to school because I didn't know if I could complete a pass in college," he admitted. "Forget about trying to be like Peyton."*
>
> "

Manning could have entered the NFL draft after his junior year, but instead he returned to Ole Miss for his senior season in 2003. "I felt like I needed to come back to become a better player," he explained. By season's end, he was very happy with his decision. He guided the Rebels to a 10-win season that was capped by a 31-28 Cotton Bowl victory over Oklahoma State on New Years' Day. "Everything about this year has been great," he said afterward. "That's the way it has been, the way the seniors stepped up and really played well together. To come to the Cotton Bowl and have your last game with all of those guys and get a win—it has been a great run."

Manning also received several prestigious awards at season's end, including the Maxwell Award, given to the nation's best all-around college football player, and the Johnny Unitas Golden Arm Award, which goes to the best quarterback. Manning also finished third in the voting for the Heisman Trophy, the best-known award in college football.

Manning finished his career at Ole Miss with 86 touchdowns and more than 10,000 passing yards. Only four other quarterbacks in conference history had broken the 10,000-yard mark in career passing yards before him. In addition, he set 47 different school records (game, season, and career) at Ole Miss.

Manning's exploits made him a sure-fire top pick in the 2004 NFL draft. Many coaches and scouts thought that Eli might have even more poten-

Manning became a star quarterback at Ole Miss, with 86 touchdowns and more than 10,000 passing yards.

―――― " ――――

Manning's exploits made him a top pick in the 2004 NFL draft. According to New York Giants General Manager Ernie Accorsi, "He elevates the play of the people around him. The majority of the teams Mississippi plays in the SEC have far better talent, but Mississippi still won 10 games [in 2003]. He makes people better."

―――― " ――――

tial than Peyton, who had emerged as a star quarterback with the Indianapolis Colts. "At this stage, Eli is much further along than Peyton," said former Mississippi State Coach Jackie Sherrill. "There is not another quarterback in the nation as good as him." New York Giants General Manager Ernie Accorsi agreed: "He elevates the play of the people around him. The majority of the teams Mississippi plays in the SEC have far better talent, but Mississippi still won 10 games [in 2003]. He makes people better."

NFL-New York Giants

As expected, the San Diego Chargers selected Manning first overall in the 2004 NFL draft. But Manning refused to play for the Chargers, a losing team with controversial ownership. The young quarterback praised the city and its fans, but most observers believe that the team's struggles convinced him that he should begin his career elsewhere. "I didn't think San Diego was the place for me to go," he said. "It was my decision, and I felt strongly about it. I knew I was going to get criticized and harassed about it, and I was willing to go through that."

A few days after the draft, the Chargers traded Manning to the New York Giants. In return, the Giants gave the Chargers quarterback Philip Rivers, who had been selected fourth overall in the draft, and three other high draft picks. The high price paid for Manning, along with his brother Peyton's success in Indianapolis, led many New York fans to demand immediate results from the rookie quarterback.

Unfortunately, Manning's rookie season with the Giants was a disappointment, both for him and for fans. He started the season on the bench so that he could watch and learn the pro game from Kurt Warner, a veteran quarterback who had won a Super Bowl a few years earlier with the St. Louis Rams. When Warner struggled at midseason, Head Coach Tom Coughlin benched him and put Manning in his place. But the quarterback switch failed to spark the team. Instead, New York lost the first six games

Manning's rookie season in the NFL was disappointing—to Manning himself, as well as to New York Giants' fans.

Manning started. He did not earn his first NFL victory until the last game of the season, and he finished his rookie year with more interceptions (9) than touchdowns (6).

Manning's difficult introduction to the NFL was made even harder by the fact that he was compared unfavorably to big brother Peyton, who fired a then-NFL record 49 touchdown passes in 2004. After the season ended, Manning admitted that he had a lot to learn. "I looked at film [of my rookie season], and I said, 'That's not me,'" he recalled. "That's not the way I've played before. That's not the way I practiced. I didn't have the answer for what was going on and why." In a smart move, Manning turned to his older brother for advice and support. "It's rare to have a best friend who is also your brother and also an NFL football player," Eli explained, "and he knows exactly what I'm talking about."

Manning studied and practiced hard in the offseason. As the 2005 season approached, he felt a renewed sense of confidence in his abilities. "I feel I know what I'm doing," he said. "It's just a matter of actually doing it." Other observers, though, wondered if the pressure of living up to the Manning name and playing in the biggest city in the country would get to him. "I cannot imagine what it's like to be Eli Manning," wrote sportscaster Joe Buck in *Sporting News* in 2005. "Can it be any fun? Think of the pressure this guy is under every time he steps on the field. Being a member of the NFL's royal family has to make each mistake hurt just a little bit more. Not only was his father a beloved figure, but his brother is now the golden boy of the league."

——— " ———

"I cannot imagine what it's like to be Eli Manning," wrote sportscaster Joe Buck. "Can it be any fun? Think of the pressure this guy is under every time he steps on the field. Being a member of the NFL's royal family has to make each mistake hurt just a little bit more. Not only was his father a beloved figure, but his brother is now the golden boy of the league."

——— " ———

Fighting Through Difficult Years

In 2005 Manning showed off the talent that had convinced the Giants to trade for him. He passed for 3,762 yards and 24 touchdowns to help lift the Giants to an 11-5 record and the NFL East division title. But Manning also threw 17 interceptions, and he suffered through a nightmarish game in his first playoff start. Facing the Carolina Panthers, he threw 3 interceptions, lost a fumble, and was sacked 4 times in a 23-0 loss. Up to that game, even the most demanding Giants fans had acknowledged that the young quarterback was learning on the job. But after the Carolina drubbing, some fans declared that New York would never win a Super Bowl with Manning at the helm.

The 2006 season started off with a bang, as Eli and the Giants faced big brother Peyton and the Colts in the season opener for both teams. Eli and Peyton thus became the first brothers ever to start at quarterback for opposing teams in an NFL game. The Giants lost the game by a 26-21 score, though, and the team struggled to get untracked all season long. New York finished with a disappointing 8-8 record, which was not good enough for a playoff berth. Once again, fans and sports media placed much of the blame squarely on Manning. Dismissing his 24 touchdown passes and his career-best completion percentage (57.7 percent), they dwelled on his 18 interceptions. They also charged that he was so soft-spoken and mild-mannered that he could not be an effective team leader.

This criticism of Manning became even greater during the lead up to the 2007 season. Tiki Barber, a star running back for the Giants who had retired after the 2006 campaign, openly questioned Manning's ability to inspire his teammates. Barber said that the quarterback's motivational speeches were "almost comical" and suggested that he did not command respect from his teammates in the huddle.

Manning's coaches and teammates defended him, and the quarterback himself tried not to let Barber's comments bother him. "You just have to learn to accept [criticism]," he stated. "You never know when it is going to happen or what is going to cause it or what strikes it up. But it is out there, and you can't let it affect your personality or the way you are in the locker room or your approach. You have to stay the same and have a good attitude about everything and show everybody that it doesn't bother you and doesn't affect you and you are going to go out there and still practice hard and perform hard."

"You just have to learn to accept [criticism]," Manning stated. "You never know when it is going to happen or what is going to cause it or what strikes it up. But it is out there, and you can't let it affect your personality or the way you are in the locker room or your approach. You have to stay the same and have a good attitude about everything and show everybody that it doesn't bother you and doesn't affect you and you are going to go out there and still practice hard and perform hard."

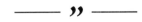

Proving His Doubters Wrong

As the 2007 season unfolded, Manning's doubters continued to criticize him. He finished the season with 20 interceptions, tied for most in the league. Critics claimed that high interception total showed that he was not maturing into a top quarterback, and they continued to question his leadership skills.

But Manning's teammates, coaches, and other supporters defended the young signal-caller. They noted that he also threw for 3,336 yards and 23 touchdown passes in 2007, even though his receivers struggled with injuries and dropped passes all season long. In addition, he did manage to

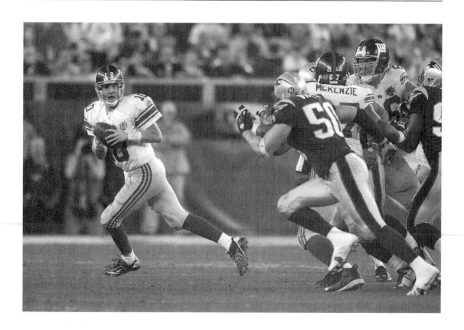

In the 2008 Super Bowl, Manning scrambles away from the Patriots' defense to fire a fourth-quarter pass to David Tyree, leading to the New York Giants 17-14 victory.

lead the Giants to a 10-6 record and a wild card spot in the 2007 NFL play-offs. They also reminded critics that in the final game of the season against the unbeaten New England Patriots, Manning's four touchdown passes almost enabled New York to pull off a massive upset.

Manning and the Giants entered the playoffs knowing that as a wild card entry, they would have to win three playoff games on the road just to reach the Super Bowl. Their first foe was the Tampa Bay Buccaneers. Manning turned in a terrific performance, completing 20 of 27 passes for 185 yards and two touchdowns, as the Giants cruised to a 24-14 victory. The Giants then moved on to play the Dallas Cowboys, who had beaten New York twice during the regular season. Once again, though, Manning's steady play helped lift the Giants to victory. He completed 12 of 18 passes for 163 yards and two touchdowns in a 21-17 victory.

The victory over Dallas put the Giants in the National Football Conference (NFC) Championship game against the Hall of Fame quarterback Brett Favre and the Green Bay Packers. The winner of this game would earn the right to play in Super Bowl XLII. At game time, most people thought the

Packers would win. The weather conditions were terrible, with heavy snow, extreme cold, and high winds out on the field, and Favre was famous for performing well in those situations. But as the game unfolded, it was Manning who seemed immune to the frigid cold and arctic winds. He outplayed Favre from beginning to end, throwing for 251 yards and rallying his team to an exciting 23-20 overtime win.

Super Bowl Champion

New York's opponent in the Super Bowl was the New England Patriots. Led by star quarterback Tom Brady, the Patriots entered the game with an 18-0 record (16 regular season wins and 2 playoff victories). Most experts expected Brady and the Patriots to beat the Giants and complete the first undefeated NFL season since the Miami Dolphins went 17-0 in 1972.

"This [victory] is about this team, about the players, the coaches, everybody who has believed in us," Manning declared. "It's not about proving anything to anybody. It is just about doing it for yourself, doing it for your teammates."

When the game actually started, though, it became clear that the Giants intended to give the mighty Patriots all they could handle. The New York defense held Brady and the explosive Patriots offense in check, in part because Manning and his offensive teammates mounted time-consuming drives. Late in the fourth quarter, though, Brady guided New England to a touchdown that gave the Patriots a 14-10 lead.

The Giants received the ball with less than three minutes to go in the game. As Manning joined his teammates in the huddle, he spoke confidently about their chances of pulling out a victory. "I said [to the team], 'This is where you want to be,'" he recalled. "I've talked to Tom [Coughlin] before and with Peyton, and … this is the situation you want to be in. You want to be down by four at the end of the game where you kind of have to score a touchdown."

As the stadium crowd screamed, Manning calmly moved his team down the field. The drive almost stalled at mid-field, but the Giants kept it going with one of the most miraculous plays in Super Bowl history. Dropping back to pass, Manning was swarmed by New England tacklers. But he somehow wriggled free and fired a pass far downfield to receiver David

Holding his Vince Lombardi trophy for Most Valuable Player, Manning celebrates during a Super Bowl parade in New York.

Tyree. The Giants receiver outjumped a New England defender for the ball, then trapped the football against his helmet with one hand. Tyree then somehow kept possession of the ball as he and the Patriot defender fell in a heap. "I knew people were grabbing me, but I knew I wasn't getting pulled down," Manning recalled. "I was trying to make a play, trying to avoid the sack. I saw [Tyree] in the middle, and the ball just hung up there forever. It was an unbelievable catch."

A few plays later, Manning fired a touchdown pass in the game's closing seconds to clinch a pulse-pounding 17-14 victory for the Giants. Fans and reporters alike immediately began debating whether the New York triumph ranked as the biggest upset in NFL history.

Manning's gutsy performance made him the obvious choice for the Super Bowl Most Valuable Player Award. He had played well all game long, completing 19 of 34 passes for 255 yards. But it was in the fourth quarter—with the game on the line—that Manning had really shined. He completed 9 of 14 passes for 152 yards and 2 touchdowns, including the game winner. "He not only made plays, he made spectacular plays," said broadcaster and Hall of Fame quarterback Terry Bradshaw.

Manning's amazing 2007 playoff run silenced all of his critics. But the young quarterback insisted that he did not spend a lot of time thinking about that. "This [victory] is about this team, about the players, the coaches, everybody who has believed in us," he declared. "It's not about proving anything to anybody. It is just about doing it for yourself, doing it for your teammates."

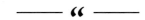

"When I call him on Tuesdays, on his off day, he is always at the facility lifting weights or studying film," said his brother Peyton. "When I call him on Wednesday nights or Thursday nights, what is he doing? He is always studying film. As a quarterback, I just can't tell you how much I appreciate that kind of work ethic, because I'm very much in the same mode."

MARRIAGE AND FAMILY

Manning married his college girlfriend, Abbey McGrew, in Mexico on April 19, 2008. They live in Hoboken, New Jersey, during the football season.

HOBBIES AND OTHER INTERESTS

Manning loves to shop for antiques, but does not have time for a lot of other hobbies during football season. "When I call him on Tuesdays, on his off day, he is always at the facility lifting weights or studying film," said his brother Peyton. "When I call him on Wednesday nights or Thursday nights, what is he doing? He is always studying film. As a quarterback, I just can't tell you how much I appreciate that kind of work ethic, because I'm very much in the same mode."

Manning also lends his time and money to a variety of charitable organizations. He and Peyton were particularly active in helping the people of

New Orleans after Hurricane Katrina struck the city in 2005. They even sent an airplane full of food, clothing, and other supplies to New Orleans. "It's hard to watch what's happened to the city, people with no place to go, up to their waists in water," Eli recalled. "We just wanted to do something extra, so we set up this plan to help some of these people."

SELECTED HONORS AND AWARDS

Conorly Trophy (Mississippi Sports Hall of Fame): 2001, 2003
All-SEC First Team (Associated Press): 2003
College Hall of Fame Scholar Athlete Award: 2003
Johnny Unitas Golden Arm Award (Unitas Golden Arm Foundation): 2003
Maxwell Award (Maxwell Football Club): 2003
Player of the Year (Southeastern Conference): 2003
Most Valuable Player, Super Bowl XLII: 2008

FURTHER READING

Periodicals

Boys' Life, Aug. 1998, p.24
Football Digest, Dec. 2001, p.34; Summer 2004, p.30
New York Times, Oct. 14, 2001, p.S5; Jan. 29, 2008, Sports section, p.1
Sporting News, Sep. 30, 2002, p.30; Mar. 22, 2004, p.12; Dec. 23, 2005, p.10
Sports Illustrated, Nov. 12, 2001, p.46; May 3, 2004, p.50; Sep. 5, 2005, p.130; Jan. 14, 2008, p.52; Feb. 13, 2008, p.66
Sports Illustrated for Kids, Aug. 2003, p.T7; Nov. 2003, p.82; Nov. 2006, p.25
Time, Dec. 5, 2005, p.95
USA Today, Sep. 23, 2005, p.C1; Sep. 6, 2006, p.A1; Feb. 1, 2008, p.C1; Feb. 4, 2008, p.C9; Feb. 5, 2008, p.C4

ADDRESS

Eli Manning
New York Football Giants
Giants Stadium
East Rutherford, NJ 07073

WORLD WIDE WEB SITES

http://www.giants.com
http://www.nfl.com
http://sports.espn.com

Kimmie Meissner 1989-

American Figure Skater
2006 World Figure Skating Champion

BIRTH

Kimberly Claire Meissner, who goes by the nickname Kimmie, was born on October 4, 1989, in Baltimore, Maryland.
She grew up in nearby Bel Air, Maryland. Her mother is Judy
Meissner; her father is Paul Meissner, a podiatrist, or doctor
specializing in treatment of the feet. Kimmie has three older
brothers: Nate, Adam, and Luke.

YOUTH

Meissner's three older brothers "probably helped shape her competitive force," said the skater's long-time coach, Pam Gregory. "She competed with them in everything." It was Nate, Adam, and Luke who first got Kimmie up on skates in 1994, after a sudden winter storm left the family's backyard coated in ice. The boys were all hockey players, so they put on their skates and started an impromptu game. They also put a pair of old hockey skates on their little sister and dragged her outside to join them. She loved it.

Before long, Meissner was taking part in the U.S. Figure Skating Basic Skills Program, which uses a carefully designed curriculum to help young skaters build strength, coordination, and technique. She started private lessons with Gregory when she was about eight years old. About two years later, Gregory became Meissner's coach, working with her five times a week at the Ice Skating Science Development Center at the University of Delaware.

> "She always wanted to go more," her mother said about Kimmie's early days in skating. "Even when we left the rink here, as we were walking out the door, she would go up to one of the coaches and say, 'Watch my spin.' She just could never have enough of it."

The skating center was about an hour drive from Meissner's home, but her parents didn't mind putting in the time and effort to get her there. They knew that their daughter had a lot of talent, and, even more important, that she loved skating. Her mother, who usually did the driving, often took a book and read during the long hours that Meissner spent training. "She always wanted to go more," her mother said about Kimmie's early days in skating. "Even when we left the rink here, as we were walking out the door, she would go up to one of the coaches and say, 'Watch my spin.' She just could never have enough of it." Still, Judy Meissner regarded skating as something that her daughter would probably only do for a few years, perhaps until she reached high school. She never imagined that Meissner's high school years would include a trip to the Olympics as part of the U.S. figure skating team.

EDUCATION

Meissner remained in public school until she was 18. She attended Hickory Elementary School and, later, Fallston High School in Bel Air,

Maryland. The demands of her skating schedule meant that she could not be in the classroom full-time, however. Between the hour-long drive each way and the time on the ice, training took up about eight hours of a typical weekday, and competitions often took her away from school for days at a time. Many young skaters are home-schooled or tutored to meet their educational requirements, but Meissner and her parents both felt that it was important for her to stay enrolled at Fallston. They wanted her to have a life that was as normal as possible, despite her skating commitments. "My family and I purposely made sure that I stayed in school," Meissner said. "I loved school. I was always happy to have that separate outlet. I wasn't just skating all the time."

Staying in school required a lot of effort and dedication. Meissner would arrive before normal class hours to work privately with some of her teachers, then spend time in regular classes with the other students. By noon, she would leave school for the day to head to Delaware for her session with Gregory. She made up for her shortened school hours with additional tutoring and online work, and she often did her homework in the car on the way to Delaware or back. When she had extended absences because of competitions, her teachers offered to tutor her in the evenings to help her catch up. She always kept her grades up, consistently getting A's and B's.

> **"My family and I purposely made sure that I stayed in school," Meissner said. "I loved school. I was always happy to have that separate outlet. I wasn't just skating all the time."**

Meissner graduated from Fallston High School in 2007. Later that year, she enrolled as a freshman at the University of Delaware, taking classes in English, psychology, and philosophy. She had been skating at the university's ice center for more than 10 years, so the campus was already like a second home to her. She was happy to take classes there so that she could continue her established routine, commuting back and forth between her parents' home and the university and rink. "It really helps after a day of skating to go back with my parents," she said. "I can just relax, unwind, and talk to them about everything." Skating commitments made keeping up with college a challenge, but the flexibility of online coursework helped her manage her schedule in her freshman year.

CAREER HIGHLIGHTS

International Competitor

When Meissner first began training with Pam Gregory, she disliked the coach's emphasis on mastering the basics. "She had me do edges and stroking. No jumps. I didn't like it, not at all. I was like, 'Let's jump,' and she would shake her head no and say, 'I need to see crossovers in a circle,'" Meissner remembered. "Now, I'm really glad I got that training, because that's what you rely on when you're out there on the ice all by yourself."

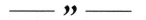

"She had me do edges and stroking. No jumps," Meissner said about her coach, Pam Gregory. "I didn't like it, not at all. I was like, 'Let's jump,' and she would shake her head no and say, 'I need to see crossovers in a circle.' Now, I'm really glad I got that training, because that's what you rely on when you're out there on the ice all by yourself."*

Under Gregory's guidance, she progressed well and eventually began entering figure skating competitions. In 2003, Meissner accomplished one of her first major skating goals—making it to the U.S. Championships. Just reaching that level of competition would have been quite an achievement, but she did more—she won the ladies' novice title.

Meissner's success at the national level spurred her on to new goals. "From there I wanted to get to Junior Worlds and then it kind of progressively got bigger," she said. Her drive to achieve paid off in the next season. She won two Junior Grand Prix medals and placed fifth at the Junior Grand Prix Final. At the U.S. Figure Skating Championships in Atlanta, she skated to the junior title. Following that triumph, she went on to the 2004 World Junior Championships, held in The Hague, Netherlands. There she landed her first triple lutz-triple toe combination jump in competition and won the silver medal, finishing second to Miki Ando of Japan.

An Incredible Jump

In the 2004-2005 skating season, Meissner moved up to the senior level of competition in the United States, but she was too young to qualify for senior status on the international level. In the Junior Grand Prix skating series that season, she won silver medals at competitions in Courchevel, France,

*Meissner placed third at the 2005 U.S. Figure Skating Championships,
when she was only 15.*

and Long Beach, California. At the Junior Grand Prix Finals in Helsinki, Sweden, in December 2004, she took the bronze medal for third place.

In January 2005, she competed in the U.S. Figure Skating Championship. Although she was only 15 years old, she placed third in the women's over-

Skating isn't as glamorous as it looks in competition; in fact, most of the sport is spent in practice sessions.

all standings. That accomplishment alone was outstanding, but her performance that year was especially memorable because she executed the demanding and difficult triple Axel jump during her program. The triple Axel requires the skater to kick off on the left foot, do three and a half rotations in the air, and land on the right foot. Only one other U.S. female skater had ever successfully done this in competition before—Tonya Harding, in 1991. "I was really excited to land that jump," Meissner remembered. "I was just doing them really well at that competition in practices, so I kind of threw it in and happened to land it." After the U.S. Championships, Meissner finished fourth at the Junior World Championships held that year at Kichener, Ontario, Canada.

2006 Winter Olympics

During the next season, Meissner turned 16 years old and became eligible to compete as a senior skater at the international level. From these ranks, Olympic team members are selected. Meissner hoped that she might make it to the Olympic Games by 2010. Her 2005-2006 season began well; she competed at two Grand Prix competitions, the NHK Trophy and the Trophee Eric Bompard, and took fifth place at both. Her performances continued to be strong as the season went on, including winning the silver medal at the 2006 U.S. Championships. Her first year in senior-level international competition had been so outstanding that Meissner was selected to be part of the Olympic team sent to the 2006 Winter Olympics in Turin, Italy.

Meissner had already done quite a bit of travel in the course of her career, but going to the Olympics was a thrill unlike any she had experienced before. Thinking back to her early years in figure skating, she recalled, "I set goals like, 'I want to go to the Olympics,' but it is different when you are actually there. Then it is like, 'Wait a minute!' You kind of do a double take. It is strange." Coach Pam Gregory noted that Meissner was excited about everything she encountered on the trip to Turin: "Every five feet, there's something about the Olympics—the rings or something. Every single thing has impressed her, from flying into town, the big welcome, the Olympic Village, going through processing to get her U.S. team gear." Meissner was probably also excited to hear that her teachers had decided to give her a three-week reprieve from homework while she was at the Olympics, so she could concentrate on her performance. In the short program part of the competition, she landed a triple lutz-triple toe jump and placed fifth; in the free skate portion, she placed sixth. Meissner came in sixth overall in the women's figure skating standings at the 2006 Winter Olympics.

2006 World Champion

As the Olympics drew to a close, Meissner came down with an illness that left her head very congested. On the flight home to the United States, the air pressure in the plane caused a complete rupture of one of her eardrums, and a partial rupture of the other. Her ears did eventually heal, but for a time, the ruptures had a negative effect on her performance. Her sense of balance was off, making it hard to spin, and she had a tough time hearing what her coach was saying to her as she skated. Nevertheless, she kept working, getting ready for her first year of competition at the senior level at the World Championships, held in Calgary that year. Her performance at Calgary was outstanding; in her free skate, she landed seven triple jumps, including two triple-triples. She was awarded the gold medal and named World Champion. Her performance at the 2006 World Championships impressed David Raith, the executive director of U.S. Figure Skating. "She had the skate of her life at the World Championships," Raith commented. "She has a great attitude and always looks for the next opportunity to show what she can do."

Being an Olympic competitor and a world champion all in one season was "awesome," Meissner said. "It was one big thing after another," It changed her life in many ways. She had a chance to throw out the opening pitch at baseball games with the Baltimore Orioles and, later, the Philadelphia Phillies. She took a televised ride with NASCAR driver Wally Dallenbach and visited the White House to read stories to children and take part in the annual Easter Egg Roll. A street in her hometown was renamed "Kimmie Way" in her honor. She signed national endorsement deals with Subway, Under Armor, and Visa, as well as a local endorsement agreement with a BMW car dealership near her home. The dealership even gave her a car of her own, but Meissner had been too busy with her skating career to learn how to drive.

> "When I won Worlds, I went from being the underdog to people expecting me to win everything I did after that," Meissner said. The pressure to maintain her extremely high level of performance was intense. "I think that was the roughest part for me, just that year afterwards. That whole year was difficult, going after every competition. I wanted to do really well, but it was just hard."

High Expectations

Meissner was on top of the world, and yet, her new level of success brought new challenges. "When I won Worlds, I went from being the underdog to people expecting me to win everything I did after that," she said. The pressure to maintain her extremely high level of performance was intense. "I think that was the roughest part for me, just that year afterwards. That whole year was difficult, going after every competition. I wanted to do really well, but it was just hard."

As the 2006-2007 season began, Meissner's first event was Skate America, where she competed against two young Japanese skating stars, Mao Asada and Miki Ando. Like Meissner, Asada had successfully landed a triple Axel in competition. Media coverage tried to build up the idea of a rivalry between the two young skaters because they were both noted for making the tough jump. According to Meissner, however, their relationship is amicable. "Mao and I are actually pretty good friends.... We did juniors together so if we go to [the same] competitions we always have fun together. I think we both push each other." Meissner won the silver medal at Skate America, behind Ando and in front of Asada.

The year 2006 was exciting for Meissner—she skated in the Olympics and won first place at the World Figure Skating Championship (shown here).

The media's emphasis on the triple Axel was another challenge Meissner had to face. She was frequently asked when, or if, she would incorporate it into her programs. It was a difficult jump that she was not consistently able to do. When she landed it at the 2005 Worlds, it was something she had impulsively added to her program. Since then, the interpretation of the scoring system had become more strict, and the more stringent style of judging makes it "kind of hard to throw in a jump," Meissner said. "If you are going to take that risk, you have to know that you are going to do it. It was different under the old system. Now you have to be pretty sure of yourself."

> According to Coach Gregory, Meissner has a good personality for dealing with the stress of international competition. "For a teenage girl, she is pretty even keel," said Gregory. "One of the reasons Meissner has had so much success is that even on frustrating days, she gets through problems much faster than if she were an emotional mess out there."

In trying to manage the intense pressure that top-level competition can bring, Meissner said she tries to avoid any feeling that the other skaters are her rivals. "I try and compete to beat my own scores.... I try not to look at it like, 'I have to beat this person or I have to be ahead of her.' That doesn't work for me." Coach Gregory commented that Meissner has a good personality for dealing with the stress of international competition. "For a teenage girl, she is pretty even keel," said Gregory. "One of the reasons Meissner has had so much success is that even on frustrating days, she gets through problems much faster than if she were an emotional mess out there."

Meissner felt the 2006-2007 season was a tough one, but she nevertheless won gold medals at the 2007 U.S. Championships and the Four Continents competition. At the World Championships, she placed fourth, placing behind Ando, Asada, and Yu-Na Kim from Korea. She also got her driver's license that year and achieved her personal goal of driving her BMW to Fallston High, just a couple of weeks before she graduated. While remaining a student there, she had traveled around the world to compete, visiting France, Italy, Slovenia, Bulgaria, Japan, and many other countries. "I've been balancing school and skating pretty much my whole life," said Meissner of her busy schedule. "It gets to be a lot and sometimes it's overwhelming because of how much work I have off the ice and then how much work I have to do on the ice." Nevertheless, she chose to continue her education along with her skating, enrolling as a freshman at the University of Delaware in autumn 2007.

A Slump in Performance

Meissner started the 2007-2008 season in good form, winning the gold medal at the Skate America competition in Reading, Pennsylvania. Soon, however, things began to unravel for her. In November, she sprained her ankle. She continued to train as best she could, but the injury certainly had an effect on her practice and her performances. At the Grand Prix Final in December 2007, she fell three times and fin-

Meissner on the winners' podium at the 2007 U.S. Championships; she took first and Emily Hughes (left) took second.

ished last. She also had three falls at the January 2008 Nationals, where she placed seventh. Some of the up-and-coming skaters who defeated her were Mirai Nagasu, Rachael Flatt, and Caroline Zhang, all just 14 and 15 years old.

In addition to her injury, the very fact of growing up presents a physical challenge to any young skater, especially a female skater. Experts say that balance and confidence can be greatly affected when the body starts to reach physical maturity. Weight distribution changes, and the body resists spinning in the way it formerly did, because its mass is not packed so tightly around its center. Skaters can try to compensate by working on more powerful launches, or by squeezing in their arms to pull their body mass closer to its center, but in any case, the female skater needs to re-learn a lot of things once her body develops. "Growing up is hard," said Michelle Kwan, a former Olympic skating champion. "You're a little off-balance. Your speed and your timing may be off. When you're at that age, you're not that confident with your body. It's an instrument, and you have to fine-tune it."

The Jump Doctor

Despite her substandard performances at the Grand Prix Final and the Nationals, U.S. skating officials selected Meissner as part of the team for the World Championships to be held in March 2008 at Gothenburg, Sweden. Her confidence was shaken from her series of falls in competition, and she actually considered turning down the opportunity to be part of the team. Instead, she took another drastic step. Many figure skaters change trainers fairly frequently, but Meissner had trained with Pam Gregory since she was a young child—for most of her life, in fact. Gregory was known as a fine coach, and had been named Coach of the Year by the Professional Skaters Association in 2006. Still, Meissner decided it was time for a change, at least temporarily. About five weeks before the Worlds, she left her Delaware skating base to go to Coral Springs, Florida, and work intensively with Richard Callaghan, a former Olympic skater himself and a trainer noted for his emphasis on the technical aspects of skating. "It was hard to say goodbye for now. Pam and I have been together forever. This is only through Worlds. After that, I don't know," Meissner said at the time. "But clearly something had to change. I couldn't go on like that."

In Florida, Meissner trained at Incredible Ice, the facility used by the NHL's Florida Panthers. Incredible Ice was also the home base for Callaghan, who had been a competitor in singles, pairs, and ice dancing during the early 1960s. In 1965, at the age of 19, Callaghan placed in the top 10 at Nationals. After he retired from competition, he spent seven years on the road with ice shows, then became a coach. One of his best skaters had been Todd Eldredge, a six-time United States champion; he had also coached top skaters Nicole Bobek, Tara Lipinski, and Shizuka Arakawa. Eldredge came to join Meissner and Callaghan for a few days of intensive work.

Eldredge and Callaghan worked on Meissner's jumps and her showmanship, but most of all, they hoped to restore her bruised confidence in herself. "It wasn't like boot camp," Meissner said of the experience. "I was working harder than I ever had, but I was having fun." The sessions included "a lot of positive reinforcement and just, you know, feeling good every day." She noted, "I got to the practice rink just wanting to skate and not feeling like I had to be perfect." The change in routine did Meissner a lot of good. At the Worlds, she took ninth place. It wasn't a gold medal, but she stayed on her feet the whole time and skated confidently. "I was happy, because it was the best that I could do and I did it," she said. "It just feels great to come back after hard performances and do something well." She wrapped up the 2007-2008 season with a strong performance at the Japan Open in April 2008 at the Saitama Super

Arena, where she took fourth place in the Ladies' Free Skate. Meissner then joined the cast of the touring show Smucker's Stars on Ice.

Meissner's goals for the future include developing more emotion in her skating, to bring maturity to the simple, athletic, technically excellent style that has taken her to the top. She hopes to be part of the U.S. team at the 2010 Winter Olympics in Vancouver, Canada, and perhaps to skate in more touring shows after that. "I am going to try and skate as long as I can," she declared. "But my family has instilled in me that there has to be something after skating. Skating is what I do for fun but I also need to have something that will be like a job." With that in mind, she may study sports medicine or physical therapy.

"I am going to try and skate as long as I can," Meissner declared. "But my family has instilled in me that there has to be something after skating. Skating is what I do for fun but I also need to have something that will be like a job."

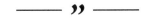

HOME AND FAMILY

Meissner's family is very important to her. Like her long-time coach, Pam Gregory, she believes that her siblings helped to propel her to skating success. "From growing up with three brothers, I am a tomboy," she claimed. "I challenge them to do everything and they are always challenging me to these big races on the ice. But, they never actually put their skates on the ice. They are too scared."

Meissner is especially close to her parents. "I can't be away from my parents too much because I love them too much," she once stated. "It makes me sad to be away from them." The 2007-2008 skating season was the first time she had traveled without one of her parents accompanying her. Meissner's parents helped her to succeed by making sacrifices to ensure that she got the coaching she needed and by giving her strong emotional support. Figure skating is a demanding sport, but her parents never pressured her to be perfect. As her long-time coach Pam Gregory summed it up, "I've come across a lot of different kinds of skating parents, and I think sometimes when people are too intense they want a return at the end.... Meissner's parents just want the return to be her happiness."

HOBBIES AND OTHER INTERESTS

When she isn't busy practicing or competing, Meissner enjoys keeping active in other ways, including running, biking, tennis, and horseback riding.

Meissner has been actively involved with Cool Kids, a group that helps young cancer patients. Among other activities, they provide supplies for kids going into the hospital, including such fun stuff as art supplies and iPods. Photo Credit: Cool Kids Campaign/Mitch Stringer.

She loves animals and has several pets, including a cat and a few dogs. She enjoys drawing, reading, and shopping with her friends. While traveling, she has collected charms from various countries, putting them on a necklace she likes to wear when skating. When putting on her skates, she always puts the left one on first, but when taking them off, she always takes the right one off first.

In 2006, after losing two friends to cancer, Meissner became involved with the Cool Kids Campaign, an organization based in Baltimore, Maryland. Cool Kids raises money to help support young cancer patients who are in treatment at the University of Maryland Medical Center and nearby Johns Hopkins Hospital, as well as other hospitals around the country. The organization gives financial help to families of patients if they need it. It hosts special outings for patients and their families. When children come in for treatment, Cool Kids supplies them with a bag containing pajamas, a journal, art supplies, an iPod or GameBoy, and other fun items. Meissner acts as a spokesperson for the organization. She has hosted a skating party for the kids in treatment at the medical centers and has put on special skating performances for them. She also designed a wrist band with the words "Cool Kids" on one side and "Triumph" on the other; it is sold to raise funds for the organization.

SELECTED HONORS AND AWARDS

State Farm U.S. Championships: 2003, Gold Medal for novice
Triglav Trophy: 2003, Bronze Medal for novice
Junior Grand Prix, Sofia: 2003, Silver Medal
Junior Grand Prix, Slovenia: 2003, Gold Medal
State Farm U.S. Junior Championships: 2004, Gold Medal
World Junior Championships: 2004, Silver Medal
Junior Grand Prix, Courchevel: 2004, Silver Medal
Junior Grand Prix, Long Beach: 2004, Silver Medal
Junior Grand Prix Final: 2004, Bronze Medal
State Farm U.S. Championships: 2005, Bronze Medal
International Figure Skating Classic: 2005, Silver Medal
Campbell's Classic: 2005, Silver Medal
State Farm U.S. Championships: 2006, Silver Medal
Olympic Winter Games: 2006, 6th place
World Figure Skating Championships: 2006, Gold Medal
Campbell's Cup: 2006, Silver Medal
Skate America: 2006, Silver Medal
Trophee Eric Bompard: 2006, Bronze Medal
Readers' Choice Award (*Skating* magazine): 2006, for skater of the year
State Farm U.S. Championships: 2007, Gold Medal
Four Continents: 2007, Gold Medal
Skate America: 2007, Gold Medal
Trophee Eric Bompard: 2007, Silver Medal

FURTHER READING

Periodicals

Baltimore Sun, Feb. 19, 2006; Mar. 26, 2006; June 15, 2006; Oct. 22, 2006; Jan. 31, 2007; Feb. 5, 2008; Mar.18, 2007; Oct. 24, 2007; Oct. 29, 2007; Feb. 5, 2008; Feb. 10, 2008; Mar. 20, 2008; Apr. 2, 2008
Chicago Tribune, Oct. 26, 2006; Jan. 21, 2007
International Figure Skating, Feb. 2007, p.11; Apr. 2007, p.18; Feb. 2008, p.32
Los Angeles Times, Oct. 27, 2006, p.D10; Jan. 24, 2007, p.D1
Philadelphia Inquirer, Jan. 30, 2006; Feb. 20, 2006; Oct. 28, 2006; Jan. 22, 2007; Jan. 23, 2007; Jan. 28, 2007
Seattle Times, Jan. 28, 2007, p.C1

Sports Illustrated, Jan. 24, 2005, p.52
Sports Illustrated for Kids, June, 2006, p.2
USA Today, Feb. 24, 2005, p.C6; Feb. 21, 2006, p.C1
Washington Post, Jan. 8, 2005, p.D1

Online Articles

http://www.baltimoresun.com/news/local/harford/bal-te.sp.meissner19
   feb19,0,6606769.story
   (Baltimore Sun, "Nice on Ice: Kimmie Meissner of Bel Air Typically Ap-
   proaches Skating with a Positive Spin," Feb. 19, 2006)
http://sports.espn.go.com/oly/columns/story?id=2391509
   (ESPN, "Unlike Other 'Shock' Stars, Meissner Here for Long Haul," Mar.
   31, 2006)
http://www.ifsmagazine.com/archive/2008/JANUARY/INDEX.PHP
   (International Figure Skating, "Kimmie Meissner: America's Newest
   Golden Girl," Jan. 2008)

ADDRESSES

Kimmie Meissner
U.S. Figure Skating Headquarters
20 First Street
Colorado Springs, CO 80906

Kimmie Meissner
Cool Kids Campaign
9711 Monroe Street
Cockeysville, MD 21030

WORLD WIDE WEB SITES

http://usfigureskating.org
http://www.bfpf.org/cool-kids-campaign
http://www.starsonice.com

Tyler Perry 1969-

American Playwright, Filmmaker, and Actor
Creator of the "Madea" Plays and Movies and the TV
Series "House of Payne"

BIRTH

Tyler Perry was born Emmitt Perry Jr. on September 13, 1969,
in New Orleans, Louisiana. His father, Emmitt Perry Sr. was a
carpenter and contractor. His mother, Maxine Perry, was a
preschool teacher. Tyler was the third of four children; he has
two older sisters and a brother who is 10 years younger.

YOUTH

Perry grew up in New Orleans in a working-class neighborhood. Two blocks north, there were mansions; two blocks

south, there were gang-filled housing projects. Living between the extremes of wealth and poverty "became my metaphor for life," he later noted. Perry faced some significant challenges growing up. Although he was a tall child, he was also sick fairly often, due to asthma. When he joined his father on a worksite, the sawdust would bring on coughing fits. He would rather play quietly at home than run around outside; reading, writing, and drawing were his preferred activities. His father, an orphan who had begun doing manual labor as a child, "understood only the physical," Perry later recalled. "He thought he could beat the softness out of me and make me hard like him." Physical abuse became a regular part of his childhood. He was harmed further when a neighbor molested him.

——— " ———

"Where I come from, you can have your dream, but keep it private," Perry related. "Don't share it with anybody, because they'll try to take it from you and snuff it out. That was the mentality of a lot of people I grew up around."

——— " ———

At school, Perry hid his pain by becoming a class clown. He expressed himself through drawing. He liked to imagine other worlds, "worlds in which I didn't worry about being poor, in which I was someone else's child, a child who lived in a mansion and had a dog." Still, he found it difficult to cope. In his early teens, he slashed his wrists, a half-hearted suicide attempt which was really "a cry for attention," he later recalled. At age 16, Perry's resentment of his father led him to change his first name to Tyler, rather than share the name of the man who beat him. Although he had big dreams, there were few people who supported them. "Where I come from, you can have your dream, but keep it private," he related. "Don't share it with anybody, because they'll try to take it from you and snuff it out. That was the mentality of a lot of people I grew up around."

EDUCATION

An unhappy teenager, Perry dropped out of high school before graduating. He later earned his General Equivalency Diploma (GED), a certification in which students must pass several exams to demonstrate knowledge equal to a high-school graduate.

CAREER HIGHLIGHTS

Discovering the Healing Power of Writing

After leaving school, Perry tried various occupations. He became a carpenter's apprentice and also worked as a car salesman and a bill collector. In 1990 he moved to Atlanta, Georgia, encouraged by the city's large community of upwardly mobile African Americans. Still, happiness kept eluding him. "The things that I went through as a kid were horrendous. And I carried that into my adult life," Perry said. "I didn't have a catharsis for my childhood pain, most of us don't, and until I learned how to forgive those people and let it go, I was unhappy." One day he was watching Oprah Winfrey's daytime talk show and heard her talk about the power of writing to help heal old hurts. He was inspired to write a journal, but because he didn't want anyone to discover he was writing about himself, he invented characters to relate his story. "That's how my first play started, which features a character who confronts an abuser, forgives him, and moves on," the writer explained.

> "The things that I went through as a kid were horrendous. And I carried that into my adult life," Perry said. "I didn't have a catharsis for my childhood pain, most of us don't, and until I learned how to forgive those people and let it go, I was unhappy."

That first play, *I Know I've Been Changed,* is about two victims of childhood abuse whose faith leads them to overcome their past. In 1992 Perry spent his entire life savings of $12,000 to rent a theater, produce the play, and act in it. It was a dismal failure, drawing only 30 people during a weekend run. One of those audience members invested in the show, however, which allowed Perry to continue pursuing his dream. The aspiring playwright worked at odd jobs over the next six years as he tried to make it in the theater. He had little success, and at times was forced to sell his belongings and live in his car. His financial troubles led to arguments with his family; during one such conflict he yelled back at his father, letting out all the feelings of anger and resentment he had kept inside for so long. The experience led him to forgive his father; "slowly but surely, I began to fuel my days with joy instead of fury," he recalled.

In 1998, Perry resolved to give himself one last chance to succeed and decided to stage his play at Atlanta's House of Blues. On opening night,

Tyler Perry as himself.

putting on his makeup in a freezing room, he felt like giving up—until he looked out the window and saw a line of theatergoers stretched around the block. "God said, 'I tell you when it's over, you don't tell me,'" Perry related. "From that moment on I've been going 100 percent. It sold out everywhere." The playwright toured with his play for the next year, performing in New York, Chicago, Philadelphia, Miami, Dallas, and Washington DC. In each city, *I Know I've Been Changed* played to sellout crowds of mostly African-American audiences.

The success of *I Know I've Been Changed* led to new opportunities for Perry. In 1999, Perry met with Dallas pastor Bishop T.D. Jakes. (For more information on Jakes, see *Biography Today,* Jan. 2005). He asked Perry to help adapt his best-selling book *Woman, Thou Art Loosed* for the stage. Perry asked for creative control, and Jakes allowed him to rewrite the play as well as produce and direct it. The play explored the conflicts between a single mother and her teenage daughter and the abuse that both must confront. The play, featuring numerous gospel numbers, earned some $5 million over a five-month tour in 1999. It made Perry a full-fledged star on the urban theater circuit, sometimes called the "chitlin circuit." This circuit refers to touring performances at theaters that cater primarily to African Americans. Historically, segregation limited black performers to such theaters, because they were banned from performing at many others. "When African Americans couldn't play certain venues, they would play this mar-

Tyler Perry as Madea, his signature character.

ket and do extremely well from the support of the African-American community," Perry explained. "It's the children and grandchildren of those
same people that will come out for you."

These first two works show just how unusual Perry is in the world of entertainment. Most entertainers hope to do just one or two things well—for
example, they might act, or act and write, or act and direct. But Perry has
done it all. While he started out as a playwright, he has also directed, produced, and acted in his own plays; adapted another writer's plays; adapted
his own plays into films; directed, produced, and acted in his own films;
written a book; and created a TV series. It's a diverse and impressive string
of accomplishments.

Creating His Signature Character

Although Perry was pleased with his newfound success, he wanted to
move away from issue-oriented drama and include more comedy in his
work. He achieved this in his next play, *I Can Do Bad All by Myself* (2000).
The play introduced the character of Mable Simmons, also known as
"Madea." (Madea, a contraction of "Mother Dear," is an affectionate nickname for grandmother in some African-American communities.) Played

by Perry in drag, Madea is a tough grandmother who is never afraid to speak her mind. "We watch with nostalgia when we think about this type of grandmother," he explained. "When she was around, everybody's kid belonged to her.... She kept the entire neighborhood straight.... She doesn't care what you think about her. She's going to tell the truth." The character was inspired by the strong women in Perry's life: his mother, Maxine; his father's mother, who shared wisdom from the Bible; and an aunt from Houston, who was rumored to carry a gun in her purse.

In *I Can Do Bad All by Myself,* straight-talking Madea has plenty to say about the love triangle between Vianne, her husband, and her sister, and the dark family secret they must overcome. Perry, who stands six feet six inches tall, had no doubts about playing the larger-than-life Madea himself. "Men watch women all the time. We sleep with you, we love you, we talk to you, we watch you shower," he explained. "I don't know if it's a Virgo thing, but I'm tuned in." Theater professionals in the Washington DC area found Perry's portrayal of Madea believable, nominating his performance for a Helen Hayes Award for Outstanding Lead Actor in a nonresident production. It was the first time this traditional Washington theater award had recognized a play staged on the urban theater circuit. With Madea's crowd-pleasing character, the play became a hit in theaters all over the U.S.

In this play, Perry established the distinctive style that has marked all his works: a mixture of comedy and melodrama, often dealing with difficult life issues, spiced with musical numbers and presented with professional production values, all communicating a message of Christian faith and forgiveness. In the character of Madea, Perry created a recurring iconic character that has appeared in many of his works, sometimes in the foreground as the main character and sometimes in the background as a subsidiary character—although Madea always manages to make herself heard. In many of his works, Madea is surrounded by her eccentric family members.

Perry continued producing a new play every year, touring to sell-out crowds all over the country. His next three plays also featured Madea, a crowd favorite. In *Diary of a Mad Black Woman* (2001), which opened in his hometown of New Orleans, the play's ending could change every night. The title character is Helen, whose husband of 18 years announces he wants a divorce so he can be with another woman—a woman who has already borne him a child. Helen gives up her middle-class comforts, moves in with her grandmother, Madea, takes a job as a waitress, and learns to move on and find love. In *Madea's Family Reunion* (2002), Madea deals with a funeral, a wedding, and a family reunion all on the same weekend.

The following year, in *Madea's Class Reunion,* Madea neets up with old friends 50 years after graduating from high school. With these plays, Perry was not only earning record box office receipts, but also millions in DVD sales. By marketing his DVDs to small urban stores, Perry found he could increase his audience. "People could see that if they spent their hard-earned money to go to my shows, they were going to have a good time."

Although Madea is a fun role to play, it can be a challenge "I have to talk high for two hours," Perry remarked, "and the costume is really, really, really hot. I'm soaking wet under there."
For his next two works, the playwright remained behind the scenes as director and producer. *Why Did I Get Married?* (2004) tells the story of several couples struggling with issues related to maintaining their relationships, while *Meet the Browns* (2005) shows a dysfunctional family trying to cope after the death of a family member. Both films found loyal audiences. In late 2005 Perry produced *Madea Goes to Jail,* in which the law finally catches up with the outrageous character. For this production he returned to the stage as Madea, but since then he has had little time for touring. He still writes and produces plays, but allows other actors to bring life to his distinctive mixes of comedy, drama, and music. In *What's Done in the Dark*

"We watch with nostalgia when we think about this type of grandmother," Perry said about the character of Madea. "When she was around, everybody's kid belonged to her.... She kept the entire neighborhood straight.... She doesn't care what you think about her. She's going to tell the truth."

(2006), Mr. Brown visits the emergency room, where staff and patients deal with various emotional problems. In *The Marriage Counselor* (2008), the title character has plenty of advice for her patients, but has trouble fixing her own troubled relationships.

Critics have given mixed reviews to Perry's plays, sometimes faulting the comedy as overly broad and the characters as stereotypes. But the author doesn't let negative reviews bother him. He was encouraged by the late African-American playwright August Wilson, author of such Pulitzer Prize-winning dramas as *The Piano Lesson* and *Fences.* "He said, 'If that's your gift, then that's what you do and do it.' Those words stuck with me." According to Perry, his theatrical specialty is "to build a bridge that marries what's deemed 'legitimate theater' and so-called 'chitlin' circuit theater,' and

I think I've done pretty well with that." His popularity and financial success as a playwright is undeniable. In 10 years, his 12 touring stage plays earned more than $150 million at the box office. Perry uses his website, more than half a million subscribers strong, to keep bringing his audience to the theater. They have also purchased more than 15 million DVDs of his plays and films.

Surprising Hollywood with Film Success

Perry's success in theater brought him to the attention of several Hollywood studios. They offered to turn his plays into movies, but only one, Lions Gate, agreed to give him complete creative control. Lions Gate, along with the BET cable channel, financed the adaptation of *Diary of a Mad Black Woman*. Perry did not direct, but he did put up some of his own money to produce the film. "This was the story I wanted to tell most because it's about infidelity, because it's about people learning how to forgive," the writer said. "It's a movie for everyone who needs information on faith, karma, and what goes around comes around. It spoke to so many situations. This is the one I wanted to be my first." *Diary of a Mad Black Woman* (2005) surprised industry experts by earning $22 million in its opening weekend, making it the No. 1 film of the week. Perry wasn't surprised by the film's performance, however. His audience, he explained, were "people who were underserved [by Hollywood], who wanted films with no gratuitous sex, no profanity, no extreme violence."

Perry made his debut as a director with his second film, an adaptation of *Madea's Family Reunion* (2006). He also played three roles in the film: Madea, her grumpy brother Joe, and her upstanding nephew, Brian. The story focuses on two of Madea's nieces, who are dealing with relationships and family expectations. For the film version, "I'm not changing anything or trying to make anything more mainstream," Perry explained. "I'm staying true to the gift God has given to me and I want to give it to people that way." Mindful that more young viewers were watching, however, he did take Madea's guns out of the story. When the film hit theaters in 2006, it scored $30 million in its opening weekend and was No. 1 at the box office for two weeks. Overall, Perry's first two films cost only $11 million to make, yet they grossed nearly $110 million in box office—a financial success that made Hollywood take notice.

For his next film, Perry produced his first original screenplay. *Daddy's Little Girls* (2007) tells the story of a mechanic who falls in love with the lawyer who is helping him fight for custody of his three daughters. Perry remained behind the camera for the film, leaving the acting to Idris Elba,

Scenes from Diary of a Mad Black Woman,
the first of Perry's plays to be made into a movie.

Gabrielle Union, and Oscar-winner Louis Gossett Jr. *Daddy's Little Girls* earned a respectable $31 million in total box office, and several critics remarked that Perry's skills as a filmmaker were improving. A *Variety* writer observed that "Perry gets better at directing every time he tries" and that his "storytelling is best when it defies convention."

Perry adapted another play for his next film, *Why Did I Get Married?* (2007). This drama about four married couples on a retreat to work on their relationships featured singer-actress Janet Jackson. Perry played the part of a pediatrician married to a busy lawyer. When it opened in 2007, it gave the writer-director another No. 1 hit, earning $21 million in its opening weekend. Because the film didn't feature his signature character, Madea, the film's success again confounded Hollywood's expectations. During its opening weekend, more people went to see *Why Did I Get Married?* than more mainstream Hollywood films starring George Clooney, Mark Wahlberg, and Cate Blanchett.

> "I look at movies where there are no African Americans at all and I go, 'Where in the world is this place where there are no black people?' I want ... people who have been ignored by Hollywood for years to get great entertainment that they can share with their families."

Perry followed that up with another successful adaptation, *Meet the Browns* (2008). There is only a brief appearance by Madea in this movie, which is a family drama and romance. Oscar nominee Angela Bassett starred as a single mother who travels to Georgia for the funeral of her estranged father and meets the family she never knew. The film became one of the all-time top 5 Easter weekend openings, earning $20 million in its first weekend of release. Perry hoped to expand his audiences with his next two films, both based on original screenplays. *The Family That Preys,* scheduled for fall 2008, features award-winning actresses Kathy Bates and Alfre Woodard in the story of a friendship between a wealthy white socialite and a working-class African-American woman. *A Jazz Man's Blues,* scheduled for 2009, is a drama set in the days of segregation.

With total box office grosses for his first five films at $242 million and growing, Hollywood is now well aware of the Tyler Perry phenomenon. In 2007 *Entertainment Weekly* ranked him No. 7 on their list of the "smartest

Perry directing and acting in Madea's Family Reunion *(top)*,
Why Did I Get Married? *(middle), and* Daddy's Little Girls *(bottom)*.

people in Hollywood." Having proven himself in independent films, Perry believed he was ready to achieve success in a more mainstream film, if he could get the opportunity. He made a start when he earned a role as the head of Starfleet Academy in the 11th *Star Trek* film, expected to be one of the biggest blockbusters of 2009.

Becoming an Entertainment Mogul

Another reason Perry has gained a reputation as one of the smartest people in Hollywood is that he has retained ownership of all his work. "I haven't sold one thing, from day one—not one song, not one show, not one script—nothing," he said, "and I will not sell a thing. I want to leave all of this to my children." By keeping control of his work, he gains a greater percentage of its profits. This has given him the money and the clout to build his own entertainment production facility in Atlanta. Tyler Perry Studios (TPS), which opened in 2006, was designed by the writer-producer himself. It has 75,000 square feet, with three soundstages for filming, a 300-seat theater, and enough room to house an acting school and a theater company. TPS is one of the country's first studios owned by an African American, and Perry is already planning an expansion that would double its size.

When Perry decided to branch out and write a book as Madea, it created a bidding war among book publishers. *Don't Make a Black Woman Take off Her Earrings: Madea's Uninhibited Commentaries of Love and Life* is filled with all sorts of common-sense advice. The subjects range from love and marriage to success and politics, with opinions told in Madea's unmistakable voice. When it appeared in 2006 it debuted at No. 1 on the *New York Times* bestsellers list, eventually selling more than 400,000 copies. It earned two Quill Awards, which promote literacy and reading, for Book of the Year and Best Humor Book. Perry's profile also increased in 2006 when he won the NAACP Theatre Awards' Trailblazer Award.

Having conquered the big screen, Perry next turned his attention to television. He created a sitcom, "House of Payne," and financed the initial run of 10 episodes himself. The story follows Curtis "Pops" Payne, a fire chief whose nephew and children move in after the nephew's drug-addicted wife burns down their house. Their clashes over the best way to raise the children provide most of the comedy. Perry cited classic 1970s sitcoms "Sanford and Son" and "The Jeffersons," both family comedies featuring African Americans, as inspirations for his show. "I want a show that really has heart, deals with life issues, and still makes you laugh," he said. When the initial run was successful, Perry signed an unprecedented deal with cable station TBS. They ordered 100 episodes of the sitcom—the equivalent of four full network seasons—for an amazing $200 million. In 2008, Perry won an NAACP Image Award for Outstanding Comedy Series for "House of Payne."

In addition, Perry has plans for a possible TV series based on his plays *Why Did I Get Married* and *Meet the Browns.* He has also signed a deal to produce 22 episodes of an animated series to feature his character Madea, targeted to a younger audience. In the long run, he aspires to own his own

A cast shot from "House of Payne."

television network. Tyler Perry's channel, he explained, would be "a network where you can turn it on with your family all day long and get positive reinforcement."

Despite the financial rewards his career has brought him, Perry stated that "I don't want to just do entertainment to do entertainment. I've never chased money. It's always been about what I can do to motivate and inspire people." If he can reach people who don't ordinarily see themselves in popular entertainment, that's a bonus, he added. "I look at movies where there are no African Americans at all and I go, 'Where in the world is this place where there are no black people?' I want ... people who have been ignored by Hollywood for years to get great entertainment that they can share with their families." He attributes his success to keeping true to his beliefs and emotions. "I come from a real place, and I come from the realness in my heart," the filmmaker explained. "People can connect to what they know, and I feel like people think they know me and I feel like I know them." In the end, Perry said, "people need laughter. They need a way to feel better. I want my work to be a mirror to motivate and inspire." He concluded: "I'm so glad that God knows what is around the corner, even when we lose hope and lose faith."

> "People need laughter. They need a way to feel better," Perry explained. "I want my work to be a mirror to motivate and inspire."

HOME AND FAMILY

Perry designed and built his own 16,000-square-foot home on a 12-acre estate outside Atlanta, Georgia. "I wanted this house to be vast. I wanted to make a statement, not in any grand or boastful way, but to let people know what God can do when you believe." He also started a company, Tyler Perry Construction, to build several other homes in the neighborhood, all worth over $1 million. After zealous fans broke into his original home, he began building another Atlanta-area mansion planned to be almost 30,000 square feet in size.

Perry is single but hopes to have a family someday. He looks at the 40-year-plus marriage of his parents—with whom he has reconciled—and knows he needs to have time to devote to a family. "I want to see this time of my life through first, because when I get to [raising children], it will become more important," he said. "When you've been through what I have, you want to know where your kids are. I want to know they're either with me or with their mama."

HOBBIES AND OTHER INTERESTS

After spending years performing his plays on the road and expanding his career into film and television, Perry has had little spare time to devote to hobbies. Even his efforts in designing his own home turned into a side business. He does enjoy spreading the wealth his hard work and success have brought him. After Hurricane Katrina hit his hometown of New Orleans in 2005, he donated $1 million to Oprah's Angel Network, to build new homes for displaced people. He also gave $500,000 to help rebuild Great St. Stephen Full Gospel Baptist Church, which was ruined by flooding.

CREDITS

Plays; Writer, Producer, and Director

I Know I've Been Changed, 1998 (and actor)
Woman, Thou Art Loosed, 1999 (author, with T.D. Jakes)
I Can Do Bad All by Myself, 2000 (and actor)
Behind Closed Doors, 2000 (author, with T.D. Jakes)
Diary of a Mad Black Woman, 2001 (and actor)
Madea's Family Reunion, 2002 (and actor)
Madea's Class Reunion, 2003 (and actor)
Why Did I Get Married?, 2004
Meet the Browns, 2004
Madea Goes to Jail, 2005 (and actor)
What's Done in the Dark, 2006
The Marriage Counselor, 2008

Movies; Writer and Producer

Diary of a Mad Black Woman, 2005 (and actor)
Madea's Family Reunion, 2006 (and director and actor)
Daddy's Little Girls, 2007 (and director)
Why Did I Get Married?, 2007 (and director and actor)
Madea Goes to Jail, 2008 (and director and actor)
Meet the Browns, 2008 (and director and actor)
The Family That Preys, 2008 (and director and actor)

Other

Don't Make a Black Woman Take off Her Earrings: Madea's Uninhibited Commentaries of Love and Life, 2006 (book)
"House of Payne," 2007- (television series; producer, writer, director)

HONORS AND AWARDS

Helen Hayes Award: 2001, for excellence in theater
BET Comedy Award (BET Networks): 2005 (two awards), Outstanding Lead Actor and Outstanding Writing in a Theatrical Film, for *Diary of a Mad Black Woman*

Black Movie Award (Film Life): 2005, Outstanding Achievement in Writing, for *Diary of a Mad Black Woman*

NAACP Theatre Awards (Beverly Hills/Hollywood NAACP): 2006, Trailblazer Award

Quill Awards (Quills Literacy Foundation): 2006 (two awards), Book of the Year and Best Humor Book, for *Don't Make a Black Woman Take off Her Earrings: Madea's Uninhibited Commentaries of Love and Life*

Image Award (NAACP): 2008, Outstanding Comedy Series, for "House of Payne"

FURTHER READING

Periodicals

Current Biography Yearbook, 2005
Ebony, Jan. 2004, p.86
Entertainment Weekly, Mar. 3, 2006, p.70; Oct. 12, 2007, p.23; Oct. 26, 2007, p.9
Essence, Mar. 2006, p.120; July 2006, p.70; Aug. 2007, p.96
Forbes, Sep. 15, 2005, p.75
Fortune, Feb. 19, 2007, p.76
Hollywood Reporter, Mar. 31, 2008
Jet, Dec. 1, 2003, p.60; Feb. 28, 2005, p.51; Feb. 27, 2006, p.32
New York Times, July 8, 2004
USA Today, Mar. 2, 2005, p.10D
Variety, Feb. 19, 2007, p.41

Online Articles

http://money.cnn.com/magazines/fortune/fortune_archive/2007/02/19/8400222/index.htm
   (Fortune, "Diary of a Mad Businessman," Feb. 14, 2007)
http://www.oprah.com/rys/omag/rys_omag_200603_aha_c.jhtml
   (Oprah.com, "Tyler Perry's Aha! Moment," 2006)

ADDRESS

Tyler Perry
Tyler Perry Studios (TPS)
541 10th Box Street
Atlanta, GA 30318

WORLD WIDE WEB SITES

http://www.tylerperry.com

Marta Tienda 1950-

American Sociologist
Pioneering Researcher of Ethnic, Economic, and
Educational Issues

BIRTH

Marta Tienda was born August 10, 1950, in Edcouch, Texas.
Her parents were Toribio "Toby" Tienda, a steelworker, and his
wife Azucena Tienda, a homemaker. Marta was the second of
their five children. The family also included older sister Mag-
gie, younger brother Juan Luis, and younger sisters Irene and
Gloria. After his first wife's early death, Toby Tienda remarried
and added another brother, Reynaldo, to the family.

YOUTH

As a teenager, Toby Tienda had come to Texas from Mexico in search of the American dream: a better life. Azucena Tienda was born in the United States, the child of Mexican migrant workers. They were willing to work hard and travel far in order to improve life for their family. Marta was just a toddler when they moved the family to Detroit, Michigan, in search of a better job. When Marta began kindergarten, she was still learning English, and she felt out of place among her mostly white classmates. Still, she tried her best to learn because her parents expected her and her siblings to make the most of their education. By the time the family bought their own house in the working-class suburb of Lincoln Park, Marta was learning to read in English.

> *The Tienda family went through some rough times. After Marta's mother died and her father lost his job, the entire family was forced to work for two summers as migrant workers. Marta and her older sister were expected to pick 20 pecks (about 40 gallons) of tomatoes every day. After working in the fields, they returned to a shack with no running water and no kitchen.*

Tragedy struck the family in 1957 when Azucena Tienda died after suffering complications during surgery. Marta was only six and never got to say goodbye to her mother; her family tried to protect the children by not telling them of their mother's death until after the funeral. Marta and her siblings returned to Texas with her maternal grandmother, but the arrangement didn't work out. Their father came for them at the end of the year, taking them to visit relatives in Mexico before they went back home. Even at a young age, Marta could see that life was much harder for her Mexican cousins. She was happy to return to Michigan with her father and siblings.

The Tienda family went through some rough times after Azucena Tienda's death. They often depended on charity for food and clothing. When Toby Tienda had trouble keeping a regular babysitter, child protection services threatened to split up the family. His marriage in 1959 seemed to solve child-care issues, but the following year he lost his steelworker job because of a strike. The entire family was forced to work the next two summers as migrant workers. Marta and her older sister were expected to pick 20 pecks (about 40 gallons) of tomatoes every day. After working in the fields, they

Mexicans who worked as migrant workers, as the Tienda family did for two summers, often are forced to live in substandard, dilapidated housing with no running water or electricity.

returned to a shack with no running water and no kitchen. The summer work allowed them to keep their house in Lincoln Park, however, and the children returned to school in the fall.

School provided Tienda with both stimulation and refuge. Because her father emphasized the importance of education, she worked hard and excelled in her classes. She especially enjoyed math and science, finding excitement in solving problems. Her teachers' encouragement was a satisfying contrast to the constant disapproval of her stepmother, who was very strict and expected Marta and her siblings to do most of the housework. When she was in middle school, one of her teachers planted the idea of going to college in her young student. "It was such a riveting moment for me that I even remember what the teacher was wearing that day. Until then, I thought that college was only for rich people." Before that day, Marta had planned on becoming a beautician, but her teacher's suggestion led her to develop bigger dreams. She resolved to become the first person in her family to go to college.

EDUCATION

At Lincoln Park High School, Tienda was an excellent student and an enthusiastic athlete. She was a member of the National Honor Society and was elected president of the Girls' Athletic Association. Despite working several jobs during her high school years, she graduated in 1968, finishing third in her class of nearly 600 students.

Tienda earned a full scholarship to Michigan State University, where she studied Spanish literature with the intent of becoming a high school teacher. She hoped to return home to Lincoln Park to teach with a passion for the subject some of her own teachers had lacked. During her student teaching assignment, however, she discovered that creative teaching methods were discouraged. She earned her bachelor's degree in Spanish in 1972, graduating *magna cum laude* (with high honors). Unsure what career would suit her best, she decided to continue her studies.

——— " ———

When Tienda was in middle school, one of her teachers planted the idea of going to college in her young student. "It was such a riveting moment for me that I even remember what the teacher was wearing that day. Until then, I thought that college was only for rich people."

——— " ———

Tienda earned a Ford Foundation scholarship that paid for graduate school and elected to attend the University of Texas in Austin. While there she discovered sociology, the study of social groups and how they behave. The field often uses math and statistics to explore important issues, such as the relationship between education and income. Although she had to take additional undergraduate classes to complete some of the requirements for the field, she earned her master's degree in sociology in 1975. She remained at Texas to work toward her PhD (doctorate or doctoral degree).

During her graduate studies, Tienda focused on the branch of sociology called demography, which explores human populations, what they're made of, and how they change. She analyzed data from government censuses, official surveys of a country's population. She explored such questions as how women who work outside the home affect the economy, or whether larger families are necessarily poorer than smaller ones. She was determined to avoid being stereotyped as a "minority" sociologist, so she made sure her studies were not focused on racial issues. She also strove to produce research and writing of the highest quality. She was proud when she earned her PhD degree in 1977 and was offered a teaching job at the University of Wisconsin.

WHO ARE HISPANIC AMERICANS?

Several different terms are used to describe people from Spanish-speaking countries. The term *Hispanic*, from the Latin word for "Spain," is the most broad; it refers to a person living in the U.S. from any of the countries where Spanish is the primary language. The terms *Latino* (masculine) and *Latina* (feminine) refer to a person of Latin-American descent who is living in the United States. Latin America includes all of Mexico as well as other Central and South American countries where Spanish or Portuguese is the national language. The terms *Chicano* (masculine) and *Chicana* (feminine) refer to a person who comes from Mexico or is of Mexican descent. The term comes from the Mexican Spanish word *mexicano*, meaning "Mexican." A person of Mexican descent who is a resident or citizen of the United States is often referred to as a **Mexican-American**.

According to the U.S. Census, Hispanic Americans are those citizens who define their origin or descent as coming from Mexico, Puerto Rico, Cuba, Spain, or any of the Spanish-speaking countries in Central America, South America, or the Caribbean. Hispanic Americans, sometimes also called Latinos, can be of any race. Some trace their ancestors to Western Europe; some to the native peoples of Latin America; some to Africans brought to the region as slaves; and some to combinations of these groups.

In the government's population survey of 2006, 44.3 million Americans, or 14.8% of the population, identified themselves as Hispanic. The majority of that group, 28.3 million, was of Mexican heritage. Puerto Ricans made up the second largest group, at almost 4 million, with another 1.5 million identifying themselves as Cuban and 1.2 million as Dominican. While 25 years ago the majority of Hispanic Americans lived in the West, in the 2000s the Southeast and Midwest saw the greatest growth rates in Latino population. By 2050, the U.S. Census estimates, nearly one in every four Americans will be of Hispanic origin.

CHOOSING A CAREER

Tienda had two pivotal experiences that affected her choice of career. The first was during college, when she got a summer job working for the state of Michigan. In northern Michigan she interviewed migrant workers to see if they qualified for food stamps, a form of government assistance. On her own time, she visited the workers in their homes, witnessing the sub-standard living conditions many migrant workers endured. She also visited the farm owners, and she was surprised to see that the growers she had considered wealthy when she was working in the fields were actually struggling to make ends meet. She discovered that an "us vs. them" mentality between growers and workers didn't help solve problems; instead, both groups needed each other. She organized a meeting between growers and workers and helped establish a day-care center for parents who worked in the fields. The experience left her determined to find a career that would allow her to find helpful solutions to everyday problems.

———— *"* ————

Tienda vowed to look for ways to help Hispanic Americans improve their lives. "Becoming a sociologist would give me that opportunity," she explained. "When you know the stories behind the numbers, then you can find ways to help people. I wanted to make a difference in people's lives by changing the rules and policies that govern them."

———— *"* ————

The second experience was more tragic, occurring shortly after she finished her graduate studies and received her doctorate. Just before she was to begin her career as a professor at the University of Wisconsin, a family tragedy struck. Her brother Juan Luis, visiting Texas for her wedding, was killed in a car accident. Only one year younger than Marta, Juan Luis had always been very close to his sister. His death cut short a promising career. He had served in the army, earned his bachelor's degree in three years, and was studying law at the University of Michigan. He was active in trying to bring more Hispanic students and professors to the university, and he also offered legal help to local migrant workers. Upon his death, Marta Tienda vowed to continue his work and look for ways to help Hispanic Americans improve their lives. "Becoming a sociologist would give me that opportunity," she explained. "When you know the stories behind the numbers, then you can find ways to help people. I wanted to make a difference in people's lives by changing the rules and policies that govern them."

CAREER HIGHLIGHTS

Helping Create a Definitive Study of Hispanics

Tienda began her career at the University of Wisconsin in 1976, starting out as an assistant professor of sociology. She had not held the position

Tienda's demographic research with Frank Bean resulted in their collaboration on The Hispanic Population of the United States, *considered a landmark reference on the subject.*

long when a group of sociologists asked her to serve as an advisor on their first-ever survey of the Mexican-American population. She helped analyze the questions they were going to ask, to make sure they were appropriate and that they would produce testable data. Her contributions to this survey helped her earn a government grant from the U.S. Department of Labor.

Tienda used the grant to analyze a new survey of the Hispanic-American population. It was the first to study all groups of Hispanics (Chicanos, Puerto Ricans, Cubans, etc.) across the country, instead of just a single group or a single area. Tienda used computers to analyze the data and compare the groups. She looked at levels of education, employment, annual income, poverty rates, and household composition (the numbers and relationship of people living together). The report she prepared set a new standard for studying Latinos and helped establish her as a talented voice in the field. She was promoted to associate professor in 1980 and to full professor in 1983.

After the government's official census in 1980, Tienda performed a similar analysis of Hispanic Americans. She worked with Frank Bean, her former professor at the University of Texas. They performed *quantitative analysis*, or performing analysis, comparisons, and interpretations of numerical data. Using quantitative analysis, they compared the 1980 data to that from previous censuses. The result was the 1987 book *The Hispanic Population of the United States*. It was the first in-depth scientific analysis of America's Hispanic population, and it is still considered a landmark reference. The book looked at differences within the Hispanic population, as well as differences between Hispanics and Anglos (whites). Unfortunately, their study showed that Hispanic Americans were falling behind Anglos in terms of schooling, jobs, and income.

At Wisconsin, Tienda continued this research using quantitative analysis. By studying census data, she could compare one moment in time to another, measuring changes in populations over time. This led her to discover that among Hispanics, economic conditions between 1970 and 1980 improved the most for Cubans. They improved to a lesser degree for those of Mexican heritage, while conditions for those of Puerto Rican heritage actually declined. This was useful information, but she wanted to explore why this had happened. In 1987 she took a position at the University of Chicago, a private university with a world-class reputation. Chicago, as the university is known, is one of the top schools in the country.

Looking for Reasons Behind the Statistics

At the University of Chicago, Tienda had the opportunity to do more in-depth research on the Hispanic experience. Because the Chicago area has

Tienda in her college office, surrounded by just a few of the many books she uses in her research. Photo Credit: Susan R. Geller, Office of Communications, Princeton University (1998).

a large local population of Hispanics, she could perform *longitudinal analysis,* or studying the same group of people over time. In this way she could explore why economic conditions varied between groups. She could also perform *qualitative analysis,* or conducting actual interviews with people. At Chicago, she began research to explore how different ethnic groups—white, black, and Hispanic—moved from school to work. She

137

———— " ————

Tienda earned a reputation as a challenging teacher who gets the best out of students by showing them how to use criticism to improve their work—even in her freshman classes. "I deliberately mixed reading materials from political interest groups, academic publications, and various types of journalism to make the point about the need to require standards of evidence to support claims."

———— " ————

discovered that Hispanics often dropped out to get jobs, which improved earnings at first but cost them in long term. African Americans tended to stay in school longer that Hispanics, but discrimination often impeded their job search. This meant they often had lower incomes than whites with same amount of education. On average, she found whites spent longer in school, but since they found jobs sooner, they earned more money over time.

Tienda also explored what role families played in the educational success of immigrants. She looked at groups of Hispanics, Asians, and African Americans. She discovered that first-generation immigrants, the ones who move to the U.S., get less education because of language and financial barriers. Their U.S.-born children, the second generation (like Tienda herself), often did best, because foreign-born parents emphasize education as the way to succeed. The next generation, however, didn't always perform as well. This seemed to happen in all groups; Tienda speculated it might be because they assimilated into American culture so well that there was less drive to succeed.

Tienda continued producing interesting work at the University of Chicago and was eventually chosen to chair the department of sociology. She took her role as teacher very seriously as well. In 1994, for instance, she went to Israel with a former student while they worked on a book. Tienda and her children lived in Tel Aviv for a few months, having their own immigrant experiences in a country where they didn't speak the language. The book was based on the Urban Poverty and Family Life Survey, which Tienda helped design and lead. The survey started with Chicago neighborhoods that had at least a 20% poverty rate; then they divided the subjects into black, white, Mexican, and Puerto Rican groups; finally, they chose randomly among the groups until they had 2,500 people. The survey was a landmark in studying poverty, for they actually went into high-poverty and high-crime neighborhoods and asked questions face-to-face.

Tienda teaching a class for graduate students on the subject of population changes in developing countries.

Tienda's work with Haya Stier analyzing this survey resulted in their 2001 book titled *The Color of Opportunity: Pathways to Family, Welfare, and Work.* They tried to answer whether poor people who live in inner-city ghettos are different from other poor families in the way they start families, receive government welfare, and find and keep jobs. In the end, they found there wasn't much difference between poor people who live in ghettos and those who live elsewhere. In general, the continuing disadvantages of poverty—lack of opportunities for good education and good jobs—make it hard for them to compete with the non-poor. The key to breaking the cycle of poverty, Tienda observed, lay in education.

Exploring Opportunities in Education

In 1997 Tienda left the University of Chicago for Princeton University, one of the country's oldest and most prestigious universities. She taught sociology and also served as a research associate at Princeton's Office of Population Research, which she headed as director from 1998 to 2002. She earned a reputation as a challenging teacher who got the best out of students by showing them how to use criticism to improve their work. In her freshman seminar, she explained, "I deliberately mixed reading materials from political interest groups, academic publications, and various types of journalism to make the point about the need to require standards of evidence to support claims." Since 1999, when she was named Maurice P. During '22 Professor in Demographic Studies, she has focused her research on college admissions and affirmative action.

In education, "affirmative action" is the name given to policies that attempt to increase minority enrollment in university programs. The Supreme Court has struck down quotas that guarantee a certain number of spaces for minorities as unconstitutional. Universities have struggled to find ways to maintain a diverse population within their student body. To explore this issue, Tienda has studied Texas's "Top 10 Percent Law," which was enacted in 1997. The law guarantees any Texas student who graduates in the top 10% of his or her high school class admission into any of the state's public universities. While this increased opportunities for students from poorer, presumably minority-heavy schools, some worried it might harm excellent students who placed just outside the top 10%.

> —— " ——
>
> *"I'm not a woman, I'm not Mexican; I'm just a sociologist. Having said that, I am also someone who was given an opportunity through ... a doctoral fellowship targeted at Mexican Americans and Puerto Ricans. I would never have gone to graduate school without that. And I think opening those opportunities, those doors, is really what we should strive for."*
>
> —— " ——

Tienda designed questionnaires for Texas high school seniors to explore how the new law affected them. She also studied data about how minority enrollment changed after the law was enacted. Her analysis showed that the Top 10% Law did give more opportunity to kids from schools that don't usually send many students to college; in addition, it didn't force those just outside the top 10% to schools out of state (her study showed they were likely to leave anyway). However, neither did the law raise minority enrollment back to levels where it had been during affirmative action days. The results surprised her somewhat. At first she had thought her study would show that affirmative action isn't the best way to promote diversity. But "when I began to look at the evidence, the possibilities and alternatives that were 'race neutral' in a society that in many ways had become race stratified, there didn't seem to be answers," she explained. "After studying the data, I concluded that there was simply no hope that an individual could break the chains of educational inequality without affirmative action." She knows there is no single solution to increasing diversity, but she is strongly against using standardized test scores, which many researchers believe tend to be racially biased and fail to predict future academic success.

Tienda's work on issues of diversity, education, poverty, and their effects on American society have brought her international recognition. She has been elected to several prestigious scientific societies, and has served as president of the Population Association of America. In 2003 the University of Texas named her an Outstanding Alumna, and also awarded a fellowship in her honor. She has served on boards of numerous charitable foundations and research councils, including the RAND Corporation (a nonprofit public policy research company) and the Jacobs Foundation (an international nonprofit that supports youth development. She considers her work with these foundations essential, since "they can afford to take risks as well as trail blaze, set standards, and study issues in ways that our government, for instance, cannot."

Tienda continues research that emphasizes the importance of education for minorities. She notes that the increasing education gap between whites and Hispanics will become more important as Hispanic population increases. While Hispanics have the highest high school dropout rate in the 2000s, they are also one of the youngest segments of American society. "Hispanics are coming of age in an aging society. Education is the bottom line," Tienda said, if they are to find good jobs to keep the economy growing. "It would be nice if we could be a color-blind society." When she thinks of herself, "I'm not a woman, I'm not Mexican; I'm just a sociologist. Having said that, I am also someone who was given an opportunity through … a doctoral fellowship targeted at Mexican Americans and Puerto Ricans. I would never have gone to graduate school without that. And I think opening those opportunities, those doors, is really what we should strive for."

HOME AND FAMILY

Tienda met Wence Lanz, a native Venezuelan, while at graduate school in Texas. They married on August 20, 1976. Their first child, Luis Gabriel, was born in 1982, while a second son, Carlos, arrived in 1989. Tienda and her husband separated and divorced in the mid-1990s; he died of cancer in 2001. With her children now grown, Tienda lives in Princeton, New Jersey, with a dog named Sancho Panza.

HOBBIES AND OTHER INTERESTS

Between research, teaching, and serving on the boards of research foundations, Tienda has little time for hobbies. She enjoys reading and names

Tienda with her two sons, Luis Gabriel and Carlos.

Nobel Prize-winner Gabriel García Márquez of Colombia as her favorite author. She also has a love of fashionable shoes that she traces to her childhood, when necessity forced her to wear ugly saddle shoes instead of shiny patent-leather styles. She likes to demonstrate that a scholar can be stylish as well as smart.

SELECTED WRITINGS

The Hispanic Population of the United States, 1987 (with Frank Bean)
Divided Opportunities: Minorities, Poverty and Social Policy, 1988 (editor, with Gary D. Sandefur)
The Color of Opportunity: Pathways to Family, Welfare, and Work, 2001 (with Haya Stier)
Youth in Cities: A Cross-National Perspective, 2002 (editor, with William J. Wilson)
Multiple Origins, Uncertain Destinies: Hispanics and the American Future, 2006 (editor, with Faith Mitchell)
Coeditor of other academic volumes and reports; author of over 100 journal articles; editor, *American Journal of Sociology,* 1991-95.

HONORS AND AWARDS

Outstanding Young Scholar Recognition Award (American Association of University Women): 1984-85

Lifetime Achievement Award (Hispanic Business Inc.): 2004
Outstanding Latina Faculty in Higher Education Award in Research and
    Teaching (American Association of Hispanics in Higher Education): 2006

FURTHER READING

Books

O'Connell, Diane. *People Person: The Story of Sociologist Marta Tienda,* 2005

Periodicals

Carnegie Reporter, Spring 2004
Hispanic Business, Apr. 2003
Princeton Alumni Weekly, Mar. 12, 2003
Princeton Weekly Bulletin, Nov. 7, 2005
USA Today, Mar. 2, 2006, p.A3

Online Articles

http://www.princeton.edu/~paw/archive_old/PAW98-99
    (Princeton Alumni Weekly, "Color and Opportunity," Mar. 10, 1999)

ADDRESS

Marta Tienda
Office of Population Research
Princeton University
Wallace Hall
Princeton NJ 08544-2091

WORLD WIDE WEB SITES

http://www.iwaswondering.org/marta_homepage.html
http://theop.princeton.edu/
http://opr.princeton.edu/faculty/page.asp?id=tienda

Justin Timberlake 1981-
American Singer and Songwriter
Six-Time Grammy Award Winner

BIRTH

Justin Randall Timberlake was born on January 31, 1981, in Memphis, Tennessee, and grew up in Millington, a town just north of Memphis. His father, Randy, played bass and sang harmonies in a bluegrass band. His mother, Lynn, was the sister of one of the other band members. Justin's parents split up when he was just a toddler, and they both remarried. Justin was primarily raised by his mother and her second husband, a banker named Paul Harless. Justin developed a very close relationship with his stepfather, but he also maintained contact with his father, who now works as a building contractor. Justin enjoys being the older sibling to Jonathan and Steven, his half-brothers from his father's marriage to his second wife, Lisa. Justin also had a half-sister, Laura Katherine, who died shortly after she was born.

YOUTH

Lynn Timberlake was fairly young when her son was born, just 20 years old. Both mother and son say they did a lot of growing up together, and they remain very close. According to Lynn, her son always responded enthusiastically to music. "When Justin was a little-bitty baby, like three or four months old, we'd sit him in those seats, like a car seat, on the kitchen counter. He'd kick his legs to the beat of the music. We'd change the music and he'd kick his legs to the new beat. We'd say to our friends, 'Dude! Look at this!' He was like a little toy," she remembered. When he was just two years old, he harmonized with music he heard on the radio.

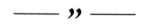

> "When Justin was a little-bitty baby, like three or four months old, we'd sit him in those seats, like a car seat, on the kitchen counter," his mother recalled. "He'd kick his legs to the beat of the music. We'd change the music and he'd kick his legs to the new beat. We'd say to our friends, 'Dude! Look at this!' He was like a little toy."

As he got older, Timberlake took singing lessons and sang in the church choir in Millington. The experience showed him how much he enjoyed singing in front of people. When he was in middle school, he and some friends entered a talent show, dressing like the popular group New Kids on the Block and singing one of their songs. The audience, composed of his classmates, chased him down the hallways, giving him his first taste of being pursued by adoring fans.

EDUCATION

Timberlake attended school in the Memphis area. He started high school there, but finished his education through a correspondence course after his career began to require frequent travel

FIRST JOBS

Timberlake began performing early in life, with his mother managing his career. He was only 10 years old when he sang at the Grand Ole Opry, a world-famous country music show in Nashville. He also won the Preteen Mr. America contest at about that time. The following year, in 1992, he was on the national TV talent show "Star Search." Performing under the name Justin Randall and wearing a cowboy outfit, he sang a country song and came in second.

The Mouseketeer Years

While taping "Star Search," Timberlake and his mother heard that auditions were going to be held across the nation to choose cast members for a television show, "The All New Mickey Mouse Club." This was an update of a popular program first produced by the Walt Disney Studios in the 1950s. In the original program, which aired every weekday, the cast wore special outfits and mouse-ear hats, sang songs, danced, and acted in skits. Cartoons and continuing adventure series were also part of the show. Each day of the week had a special theme, and adult "Mouseketeers" were there to guide the younger cast members and offer advice about life.

The "Mickey Mouse Club" was so popular that it was shown in reruns for years after the original run ended. In 1977, it was revived with a new cast as the "All New Mickey Mouse Club," but it wasn't very successful and was cancelled in 1979. Ten years later, Disney tried again. The 1989 version was officially titled "The All New Mickey Mouse Club" but was usually called MMC."

"MMC" was filmed at the Disney-MGM complex in Orlando, Florida. Featuring a talented cast of teenagers, it was made up of comedy skits, live music performed for a studio audience, pre-recorded videos by the cast, and a continuing serial called "Emerald Cove." In the original "Mickey Mouse Club," older cast members were replaced by younger ones as they became too mature to fit the show's image. The same formula was followed with "MMC," which was successful enough to stay in production for several years. During the year Timberlake auditioned to become one of the new cast members, he was one of 30,000 kids who tried out for the show. Out of all those auditions, only seven new cast members were chosen—and 12-year-old Justin was one of them. He and his mother moved to Orlando, where the show was filmed. He was part of the "MMC" cast from 1993 to 1995.

With the MGM/Disney studio, Nickelodeon studios, and many theme parks all located in the Orlando area, it was an intense place for young, tal-

A cast shot from "MMC," including Timberlake (back row, right), Christina Aguilera (middle row, right), and Britney Spears (front row, right).

ented people to meet and make connections. Timberlake's fellow "MMC" cast members included many who would go on to stardom, including singers Christina Aguilera and Britney Spears; actor Keri Russell, who starred in the television show "Felicity"; actor Ryan Gosling, who was later nominated for Academy and Golden Globe Awards; and singer J.C. Chasez, who, along with Timberlake, would become part of the sensationally successful singing group *N Sync.

CAREER HIGHLIGHTS

Forming *N Sync

Once "MMC" was cancelled, Timberlake and his mother headed back to the Memphis area, where he returned to his high school. He wasn't happy about going back to normal life, but it didn't last for long. He and fellow Mouseketeer J.C. Chasez had been working on some demo recordings. Eventually, Timberlake returned to Orlando to record solo material and try to make a deal for a recording contract. As he was working on that project, though, he and Chasez were recruited to be part of an all-male singing group that was being developed at that time.

*N Sync was no overnight sensation, but the product of a lot of hard work and planning. The other members were mostly drawn from the big pool of young talent that congregated in Florida. The band included Justin Timberlake, Christopher Alan Kirkpatrick (Chris), Joseph Anthony Fatone Jr. (Joey), James Lance Bass (Lance), and Joshua Scott Chasez (JC). The name *N Sync was created by Timberlake's mother, by using the last letters of each band member's first name. But the band name was created before Lance replaced an earlier group member named Jason. Since they liked the name, they hired Lance but jokingly referred to him as Lansten so the name would still make sense.

> **"**
>
> *The year Timberlake auditioned to become one of the new "MMC" cast members, he was one of 30,000 kids who tried out for the show. Out of all those auditions, only seven new cast members were chosen— and 12-year-old Justin was one of them.*
>
> **"**

With Lynn Timberlake acting as their manager, the members of *N Sync began to work on their choreography and harmonies. Using an empty warehouse as a studio, they would practice for hours. In the fall of 1995, they had their first gig, at a nightclub located in Walt Disney World. A friend who had worked as a cameraman on "MMC" taped their performance, and they used that recording as a demo to send out to agents and recording companies. In 1996, the tape came to the attention of Louis J. Pearlman, a business manager with Trans Continental Records. His clients included the Backstreet Boys, a hugely successful singing group at that time. Pearlman mentioned *N Sync to an associate, Johnny Wright, who also worked with the Backstreet Boys and had previously managed another singing sensation, New Kids on the Block.

At first, Wright felt that he didn't want to take on another group, one that seemed to have a lot of similarities to the Backstreet Boys. When he saw them in person, however, he changed his mind. "They could really sing," he said. "They had a chemistry—an aura about them. When they talked to

*The members of *N Sync (clockwise from upper left): Timberlake, JC Chasez, Chris Kirkpatrick, Joey Fatone, and Lance Bass (center).*

me they talked to me as a group, as a unit, rather than five individuals trying to pitch themselves to me—they weren't selfish." Wright and Pearlman agreed to sign *N Sync to a record deal with the BMG recording company.

Record company executives began looking for new music to expand the group's sound, and they decided to follow the same course with *N Sync that they had used to bring the Backstreet Boys to the peak of success. This involved taking the band to Europe for extensive on-the-road experience. They could work out any kinks in their performance, build up a European following, and bring them back to the United States to debut as a polished act. When their music was released overseas, the singles "I Want You Back" and "Tearin' Up My Heart" immediately went platinum, and their first album quickly rose to the top spot on the record charts. As the five boys took their show through Mexico, Africa, Asia, Europe, and Canada, they were playing to sell-out crowds. But when the tour ended in 1998, they returned to the United States still virtually unknown in their own country.

"They could really sing," manager Johnny Wright said about *N Sync. "They had a chemistry—an aura about them. When they talked to me they talked to me as a group, as a unit, rather than five individuals trying to pitch themselves to me—they weren't selfish."*

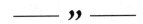

*N Sync Hits the U.S.

Their first U.S. album, titled *N Sync,* was released in spring 1998. It included "Tearin' Up My Heart" and "I Want You Back," already hits overseas. In the United States, though, the boys had to work hard to get recognition. They made appearances at radio stations, record stores, and even shopping malls to draw attention to their music. They got a big break in July of that year, when the Backstreet Boys were unable to fulfill a commitment they had made to sing for an "In Concert" special to be filmed at Disney World for the Disney Channel. *N Sync filled in for the Backstreet Boys in a show that featured their music as well as interviews with group members and footage of them enjoying Disney World with their families.

The "In Concert" special was rerun frequently on the Disney Channel after its initial airing, which gave *N Sync a lot of exposure and built up their popularity. Fans started calling radio stations requesting their music, asking for their videos to be shown on MTV, and begging for articles to be written about them in teen magazines. They began to get bookings for major television appearances, such as "The Tonight Show," "Live with Regis and Kathie Lee," and the Miss Teen USA Pageant. They were featured performers in the Macy's Thanksgiving Day Parade in New York City, and they served as the opening act for Janet Jackson on her sold-out "Velvet Rope" tour.

Their first CD confirmed the band was a hit, selling more than 10 million copies.

After a somewhat slow start, the *N Sync album built to a huge success. It had four No. 1 singles and sold more than 10 million copies. The group quickly followed up on their wave of popularity by releasing *Home for Christmas* in November 1998. This album featured new music written just for the group as well as some traditional holiday favorites.

*N Sync's appeal rested on many factors. The members were all solid performers, and the group featured tight harmonies and a wide vocal range and variety of singing styles. They could perform high-powered dance music but also be convincing in slow ballads. Their well-practiced choreography was just one aspect of an exciting stage show that included lots of special effects, costume changes, acrobatics, and a spectacular light show. The boys' good looks didn't hurt the band's appeal, while they also seemed like ordinary guys. As Timberlake said at the time, "I think there's a sense of reality that surrounds us. We don't try to make ourselves do cute, we just are who we are. We're boys. We burp and fart, just like boys."

Timberlake was the youngest member of the group. At the time he went by several nicknames including Baby, Curly, and Mr. Smooth. He has admitted that fame changed him—and not always in good ways. "I thought I was the coolest guy," he said of the period after he first signed his recording contract. "You couldn't talk to me. Nobody could tell me anything." Once *N Sync's fame was firmly established, he realized how much influence he had over other people. "We were playing stadiums, and I could say, 'Hey, we should fly down!' and suddenly people are building rigs for us to fly down on. We had a blast doing it, but I was really a perfectionist."

Taking Control: *No Strings Attached*

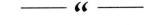

*N Sync was selling millions of albums and making a tremendous amount of money. But when band member Chris Kirkpatrick asked their managers for more of his share, he was informed that, in fact, he owed money to the management. That announcement sparked the group to review the agreements they had signed with Pearlman and Trans Continental Records. The group discovered that the contract granted Pearlman control of the band's name, 75 percent of all

"I think there's a sense of reality that surrounds us," Timberlake said at the time. *"We don't try to make ourselves do cute, we just are who we are. We're boys. We burp and fart, just like boys."*

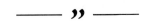

record royalties, 100 percent of music publishing royalties, 80 percent of all merchandising revenue, and 55 percent of earnings from celebrity endorsements and touring revenue. After Pearlman took his share, the remaining earnings were supposed to pay for the band's expenses before being split among the five of them.

In September 1999, the band told Pearlman that the contract was unfair and they wanted to change it. The agent's response was to file a lawsuit against them for $150 million. The band fought back with a $25 million countersuit. In December, a settlement was reached that terminated Pearlman's control over the band while granting him a share in their future profits. They were allowed to continue using the name *N Sync, but they moved to a new record label, Jive Records. They were also granted much more creative control over their music.

——— " ———

Timberlake has admitted that fame changed him—and not always in good ways. "I thought I was the coolest guy," he said of the period after he first signed his recording contract. "You couldn't talk to me. Nobody could tell me anything."

——— " ———

In 2000, they released the album *No Strings Attached.* *N Sync was so hot at the time that the record sold two million copies in its first week of sales. The title of the album expressed their feeling of freedom after escaping Pearlman's control. It also poked fun at a criticism sometimes expressed about the band: that they were over-managed and overproduced, and really not much more than a collection of pretty faces.

In the stage show for *No Strings Attached*, the boys descended from above the stage on puppet strings, which they then struggled to break. The album again contained a mix of danceable tunes and ballads, but it had a more urban feel and showed a broader range of influences, including hip-hop and old-school R&B. The *No Strings Attached* tour was a sellout in every venue, with more than a million tickets sold in six months. In 2001, the band released *Celebrity*, which didn't quite reach the heights of *No Strings Attached,* but still sold 1.8 million copies in its first week of sales. *Celebrity* was the last CD released by the group. In total, *N Sync has sold more than 27 million records.

Developing a Solo Career: *Justified*

In 2002 Timberlake branched out on a solo career, although *N Sync never officially broke up. At the MTV Video Music Awards in August 2002, he danced his way out of a gigantic boom box to sing "Like I Love You." The style of the song, his dance moves, and even the fedora hat he wore strongly suggested the influence of Michael Jackson, whose music Timberlake has acknowledged as a major inspiration.

In his solo work, Timberlake was reaching for a more mature sound that featured urban and R&B influences. He got help from the music producers Timbaland and the Neptunes. In late 2002, he released a solo album, *Justified*, to mixed reviews. Some critics dismissed it as lightweight pop, while others were impressed with Timberlake's development of an edgier sound. Fans expressed their support by buying more than three million copies of the album and flocking to see Timberlake on the *Justified and Stripped* tour,

Timberlake's appearance at the 2002 MTV Video Music Awards marked his debut as a solo artist.

which put him on a double bill with his former "MMC" co-star, Christina Aguilera. Timberlake eventually won two Grammy awards for his work on *Justified,* one for Best Pop Vocal Album and one for Best Pop Vocal Performance, for the single "Cry Me a River."

——— **"** ———

"Artie's sort of a nerd," **Timberlake commented about** *his* **Shrek** *character. "He is told his whole life that he's a loser, so he doesn't believe in himself, doesn't believe he can be the king. He's got to get confidence. He's not cool, you know?"*

——— **"** ———

Controversy and Negative Publicity

The year 2002 was a pivotal point in Timberlake's music career and in his personal life. During this period—in fact, ever since he first became famous—Timberlake has had to deal with tremendous public fascination with his personal life. He was involved in several events around this time that contributed to a wave of negative publicity. One cause was his relationship with Britney Spears. He had known Spears for about 10 years, since they had worked together on "MMC." In addition to being friends, the two of them were romantically involved for quite a while, although they had kept it out of the public eye as much as possible. In 2002, their long-standing relationship ended amid a swirl of nasty rumors. Timberlake refused to say much about his relationship with Spears or what had ended it, although "Cry Me a River" is widely thought to be about their breakup.

After Timberlake and Spears split up, he got a lot of publicity for a series of brief relationships with high-profile women, whom he usually refrained from discussing. He also got some bad publicity from the MTV show "Punk'd," in which the host, Ashton Kutcher, played elaborate pranks on people. In 2003, "Punk'd" filmed men going to Timberlake's house dressed as federal agents. They told the singer that he owed the government hundreds of thousands of dollars in taxes. Timberlake was completely taken in by the prank and was visibly fighting back tears.

More negative publicity came from the events at the Super Bowl in February 2004, when Timberlake performed at half-time with Janet Jackson. In a choreographed move, he tore at Jackson's costume and a whole section of her costume came off to reveal her breast. Many viewers were deeply offended by what appeared to be a flagrant act, although all involved swore that it was an accident. Timberlake issued a public apology for his part in

Timberlake voiced the character of Artie in Shrek 3.

the show. Jackson later suggested that the stunt had been intentional, but Timberlake maintained he hadn't known anything about it in advance. The incident led to a record fine of $550,000 from the FCC against CBS, the network that broadcast the Super Bowl.

More trouble came in November 2004. At the time, Timberlake was in a romantic relationship with actress Cameron Diaz, which he hadn't tried to keep secret. They were often followed by paparazzi (photographers who try to get candid shots of celebrities). One night while they were still a couple, Timberlake and Diaz were surprised by two photographers. There was a scuffle, Timberlake got physical, and the photographers ended up suing the two stars. The case was eventually settled out of court.

Commenting on the relentless public interest in his life, Timberlake said: "I've run the gamut with how I feel about it. I had the confrontation, where I slapped a paparazzo, and that was bad. I had to go meet the district attorney, who slapped the back of my hand and said I shouldn't retaliate with violence. I was like, 'Of course. You're right.' We live in an interesting time where everybody and everything is completely accessible. And I love what I do, but I also love my life and my privacy."

A Change in Direction

By 2004, Timberlake's career had been in high gear for several years. His father advised him to take some time off, and he agreed. "This is what

—— " ——

"I write about what I know, but I also write about things that are just fantasies in my head," he said. "I don't really think I brought sexy back. It just seemed like something catchy to say. I don't really think of myself that way. It's just fun. It's like acting, because you create a character in your mind, and you run with it."

—— " ——

the world looks like at a regular pace," he observed then. "That was amazing for me. Just the little things, like sitting home on the weekend or making a Sunday tee time. Play golf, then come back home, have a beer and call it a day."

Timberlake took some time to branch out into acting. Besides his skit work on "MMC," he had already played small roles in a few television programs, including "Switch," "Touched by an Angel," "Longshot," and hosting "Saturday Night Live." In 2000, he played opposite Kathie Lee Gifford in the made-for-television movie *Model Behavior.* He worked with top stars Kevin Spacey and Morgan Freeman in *Edison Force,* playing the part of an investigative reporter. After premiering at the Toronto Film Festival in September 2005, the film got mediocre reviews and went straight to DVD. Timberlake won praise for his work in *Black Snake Moan* (2006), in which he portrayed a soldier who suffers from panic attacks, and in *Alpha Dog* (2006), in which he played a dim-witted thug who helps a drug dealer kidnap a customer's brother in order to force payment of a debt.

Timberlake added a major hit movie to his resume when he joined the cast of *Shrek the Third,* in which he played the young King Arthur, or Artie. "Artie's sort of a nerd," Timberlake commented about his *Shrek* character. "He is told his whole life that he's a loser, so he doesn't believe in himself, doesn't believe he can be the king. He's got to get confidence. He's not cool, you know?" Even though Timberlake might seem to some people to define the word "cool," he said that he could definitely understand Artie's character. "I have my moments," he said. "We can all relate to adolescence, when nobody's cool. I used to get picked on all the time. I had terrible acne, weird hair. My arms were too long."

FutureSex/LoveSounds

During this time off, Timberlake was also working on music. In May 2004, he had surgery to remove some nodules from his vocal chords. By the end of 2004 he began working on his next album, which wasn't released until

On FutureSex/LoveSounds, *Timberlake worked with a wide array of noted producers who helped him stretch his musical boundaries.*

September 2006. He also collaborated on projects with other musicians, including Snoop Dog and 50 Cent, did backup vocals for Charlie Wilson and Black Eyed Peas, and appeared in videos by Johnny Cash and Nelly Furtado. He wrote the songs "Okay" and "Get Out" for Macy Gray, "Rehab" for Rihanna, and collaborated on "The Only Promise That Remains" with country singer Reba McEntire.

In July 2006, Timberlake released "SexyBack," the first single from his second solo album, titled *FutureSex/LoveSounds*. Like the other tracks on the album, it had grown out of his collaboration with Timbaland, who co-produced it with Timberlake and with Nate "Danja" Hills. *FutureSex/LoveSounds*, released in full in September 2006, continued to expand Timberlake's musical boundaries. Even more than *Justified*, it featured an urban sound, with a lot of techno beats and little of his famous high falsetto. "It didn't sound like Justin vocally," admitted Barry Weiss, head of Jive Records. "It was a bit of a risk for all of us. But it was a risk that clearly paid off."

At the 2006 Grammy Awards, Timberlake won two awards, for Best Rap/Sung Collaboration (with T.I.), for "My Love," and for Best Dance Recording, for "SexyBack." He followed that up at the 2007 Grammy Awards with two more awards, for Best Male Pop Vocal Performance, for "What Goes Around … Comes Around," and Best Dance Recording, for "LoveStoned/I Think She Knows." As of late 2007, the album had sold more than eight million copies, boosting Timberlake's total album sales as a solo artist to well over 15 million.

After the release of *FutureSex/LoveSounds,* Timberlake toured extensively to support the new record, appearing in concert around the world in 2007 and 2008. He also found time to collaborate with Madonna on the single "4 Minutes" and to make an appearance in the 2008 movie *The Love Guru,* starring Mike Myers.

Discussing his lyrics and his music in general, Timberlake said that it isn't all a direct reflection of his life, and that it has to be looked at light-heartedly. "I write about what I know, but I also write about things that are just fantasies in my head," he said. "I don't really think I brought sexy back. It just seemed like something catchy to say. I don't really think of myself that way. It's just fun. It's like acting, because you create a character in your mind, and you run with it." Trying to describe how he really sees himself, he offered: "I think my style is kind of a cross between a skater hippie and an R&B singer."

New Ventures

At an age when some people still haven't decided on a career, Timberlake has already had a long one. His success has been great, but there have been low points, too. While show business has provided him with many incredible experiences, he doesn't see it as something he wants to stick with forever. He has spent so much time in the spotlight that he doesn't really crave it any more. "Ten years from now," he commented, "I don't want to be jumping around onstage. I've been in this business for 15 years—which is kinda creepy—and I'm interested in other things."

In the future, Timberlake sees himself writing more music for other performers, which he views as a means of expressing himself more fully, using

Timberlake and Timbaland in a sizzling performance of "SexyBack" at the MTV Video Music Awards.

others' voices. "I want to write country music, because that's where I grew up—Tennessee. Soul music.... I want to be involved in hip-hop. And sometimes I feel the only way to really express all those different sides, even just for myself, is [by writing songs for] different people."

HOME AND FAMILY

Timberlake, who is single, has homes in Orlando and in the Hollywood Hills. He remains close with his family, especially his mother. He enjoys going home to Tennessee and having his grandmother cook for him.

FAVORITE MUSIC

Some of the musicians who have most influenced Timberlake include Michael Jackson, Stevie Wonder, Donnie Hathaway, Al Green, Marvin Gaye, the Eagles, and the Beatles. His favorite newer artists include Bjork, Avril Lavigne, John Mayer, the Strokes, the Killers, Arcade Fire, Radiohead, and Coldplay.

HOBBIES AND OTHER INTERESTS

Timberlake enjoys a variety of sports, including playing basketball, snowboarding, and surfing. He collects sports jerseys and enjoys owning several cars, motorcycles, and jet skis. He is involved with charitable activities, too. In 2000, he founded the Justin Timberlake Foundation, a music education program serving needy children. He loves playing golf, and in 2008 he began a five-year stint hosting a PGA charity tournament in Las Vegas, the Justin Timberlake Shriners Hospital for Children Open.

Timberlake has also started up a few business ventures. Tennman Records is his own production company. He has opened several restaurants, including one in Manhattan called Southern Hospitality. It features barbeque and other down-home recipes, including some from Timberlake's grandmother, Sadie Bomar. One of the singer's partners in that restaurant is Trace Ayala, a friend since childhood. Ayala designed costumes for *N Sync, and he is also one of Timberlake's partners in a line of designer clothing called William Rast, featured at upscale department stores.

SELECTED CREDITS

Recordings with *N Sync

*N Sync, 1998
Home for Christmas, 1998
No Strings Attached, 2000
Celebrity, 2001

Solo Recordings

Justified, 2002
FutureSex/LoveSounds, 2006

Television

The All New Mickey Mouse Club, 1993-1994
Model Behavior, 2000

Films

Edison Force, 2005
Black Snake Moan, 2006
Alpha Dog, 2006
Southland Tales, 2006
Shrek the Third, 2007
The Love Guru, 2008

SELECTED HONORS AND AWARDS

American Music Awards: 2003, Favorite Pop/Rock Album, for *Justified*;
    2007 (two awards), Favorite Male Artist; Favorite R & B/Soul Album, for
    FutureSex/LoveSounds
BRIT Awards: 2004 (two awards), Best International Male Artist, Best In-
    ternational Album, for *Justified*; 2007, Best International Male Artist
Grammy Awards: 2004 (two awards), Best Pop Vocal Album, for *Justified*;
    Best Male Pop Vocal Performance, for "Cry Me a River"; 2007 (two
    awards), Best Dance Recording (with Timbaland), for "SexyBack"; Best
    Rap/Sung Collaboration (with T.I.), for "My Love"; 2008 (two awards),
    Best Male Pop Vocal Performance, for "What Goes Around … Comes
    Around," and Best Dance Recording, for "LoveStoned/I Think She
    Knows"
Emmy Award: 2007, outstanding original music and lyrics, for "Dick in a
    Box"
Teen Choice Awards: 2007 (two awards), Choice Music-Male Artist;
    Choice Music-Payback Track

FURTHER READING

Books

Biography Today, 2001 (entry on *N Sync)

Periodicals

Entertainment Weekly, Sep. 20, 2002, p.36; Feb. 9, 2007, p.32
Fort Worth Star-Telegram, Mar. 2, 2007, p.32
New York Post, Jan. 7, 2007, p.36
New York Times, Oct. 22, 2006, section 9, p.1; Dec. 23, 2006, p.B11
Newsweek, Apr. 5, 2004, p.56
People, Feb. 8, 1999, p.93; June 24, 2002, p.58; Nov.11, 2002, p.73; Aug. 6,
    2007, p.70
Teen People, Dec.1, 2002 p.92
USA Today, May 1, 2007, p.D1
WWD, Aug. 22, 2005, p.8

ADDRESS

Justin Timberlake
Jive Records
137 West 25th Street
New York, NY 10001-7200

WORLD WIDE WEB SITES

http://www.justintimberlake.com
http://www.tennmanrecords.com

Lee Wardlaw 1955-
American Writer for Children and Young Adults
Author of *101 Ways to Bug Your Parents* and *101 Ways to Bug Your Teacher*

BIRTH

Lee Wardlaw was born Lee Anna Wardlaw on November 20, 1955, at the Smoky Hill Air Force Base Hospital in Salina, Kansas. Her father, Joseph Patterson Wardlaw, was a captain in the Air Force and a professional photographer who ran the photo lab on the base. He and her mother, Margaret Laux Wardlaw, had degrees in business from Ohio University. Lee remembers her father proudly saying that her birth "only cost him and my mother $7.62, as the rest of the tab was picked up by the United States Air Force." She has two younger brothers, Scott and John. Her married name is Lee Wardlaw Jaffurs, but she uses Lee Wardlaw for her pen name.

YOUTH

Wardlaw moved with her parents to Erie, Pennsylvania, when she was less then a year old. Her parents owned and operated WLEU, a radio station there. In 1960, they purchased another station, KIST radio in Santa Barbara, California, where Wardlaw grew up.

> "You could almost always find me holed up in my room with paper and pencil," Wardlaw said. "All through elementary school and high school I wrote poems, songs, stories, even my own magazine—complete with articles, ads, and an advice column. I also wrote a silly soap opera with multiple daily episodes that I secretly passed to my best friend during class."

Writing Her First Book

Wardlaw wrote her first book as a seven-year-old second grader for her school's spring art festival. The book was called *Teena Bell*, about a little girl who was only one-inch high. Wardlaw modeled the character after Tinkerbell from *Peter Pan* and Thumbelina from a story by Hans Christian Anderson. Teena Bell "looked just like me—skinny, brownish hair, crooked smile—only shorter," Wardlaw wrote on her website, www.leewardlaw. com. She has also said that "One of the reasons I made Teena Bell so small was because I wanted to grow up to look like Tinkerbell and I wanted to marry Peter Pan. I had a mad crush on him!"

Teena had a grasshopper for a best friend and 14 baby brothers and 14 baby sisters, all of whom were still in diapers. "My brother John had just been born, so I was expected to do a lot of diaper duty. Ha!" she wrote. Her mother typed up the book and bound it in a bright red report cover.

After she finished *Teena Bell,* Wardlaw continued to write. As a third grader, she created a play about an 11-year-old girl who meets the Beatles and then gets to join the band. She was taking guitar lessons at the time, which inspired the story. When Wardlaw turned 11 herself, her parents got a di-

Wardlaw enjoying a book at an early age.

vorce, which she described on her website as the worst thing that has ever happened to her. In the sixth grade, she and three girlfriends formed a rock band called the Shooting Stars. She played the guitar and wrote many of the songs that the band performed.

Wardlaw kept herself busy through good and bad times by writing. "You could almost always find me holed up in my room with paper and pencil," she said. "All through elementary school and high school I wrote poems, songs, stories, even my own magazine—complete with articles, ads, and an advice column. I also wrote a silly soap opera with multiple daily episodes that I secretly passed to my best friend during class."

EDUCATION

Wardlaw attended Santa Barbara High School, where she contributed to the literary magazine and was captain of the drill team. After graduation, she enrolled in California Polytechnic State University in San Luis Obispo, California. She earned a Bachelor of Arts (BA) degree in elementary education, also earning her teaching credential. She graduated with honors from Cal Poly in 1977.

Losing Her Childhood Home to Fire

Wardlaw experienced a personal trauma during the summer before she graduated from college when her family's home in Santa Barbara burned down. It started after a kite became entangled in some power lines, sending sparks into the dry weeds below. Despite the best efforts of firefighters, the resulting blaze burned for more than 24 hours and destroyed 200 homes. "My family's home was one of those that burned to the ground," Wardlaw recalled. "We lost everything—including my cat. Days later, while sifting through the wreckage and ash, I found only two recognizable items: a blackened baby spoon and our front door knob! I kept both as souvenirs of what I call the 'before time.'" Years later, Wardlaw used her memories of the blaze in her novel, *Corey's Fire*.

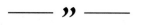

"My family's home was one of those that burned to the ground," Wardlaw recalled. "We lost everything—including my cat. Days later, while sifting through the wreckage and ash, I found only two recognizable items: a blackened baby spoon and our front door knob! I kept both as souvenirs of what I call the 'before time.'"

FIRST JOBS

Wardlaw began her teaching career at the Los Ninos Head Start early education program in Santa Barbara, California. She continued teaching for the next five years, first at the pre-school and then at an elementary school in Santa Barbara. She also worked as a tutor and served as the "tooth fairy" for a dental foundation. "There was no magic wand or tutu," Wardlaw remarked. "I drove the Brush Bus—a mobile dental education classroom." She drove the bus to area schools and gave 30-minute lessons on tooth care in the bus. She had to quit when her dentist said she was wearing away the enamel on her teeth from giving tooth-brushing demonstrations all day.

During her years as a teacher, Wardlaw continued to write in her spare time. She often watched the clock all day, she once admitted, waiting for the time when she could go home and resume writing. She knew she wanted to be a children's author, she explained, because "I have total recall of my childhood, not just what I did, but the emotions I felt. Childhood is a series of firsts and the wonder, the embarrassments, the traumas, and the tribulations are timeless. If you can remember what it felt like when you were a kid, you can connect with the kids of today."

CAREER HIGHLIGHTS

Becoming an Author

Wardlaw's path to becoming an author took some twists and turns, and she wrote for many years before she became successful. Her first published book was *Me + Math = Headache* (1986), a beginning chapter book that she started writing when she was a 19-year-old college student. The first sentence of the book is "I flunked another math test today." Those very words were "something my mother heard a lot from me when I was in elementary school, junior high school, high school," Wardlaw recalled. The manuscript was rejected by many publishers before it was finally published in 1986.

Since that time, Wardlaw has continued to write in a wide variety of forms. She has written for children of all ages, including picture books for the youngest children, easy readers and beginning chapter books for those just beginning to read independently, and novels for middle-grade readers and young adults. In addition, she has written several non-fiction books for this older age group as well. Many of these books show the humor in growing up, both in funny and in more difficult situations, and they often feature determined, goal-driven characters that work hard to achieve their goals.

> "[Corey's Fire] *took nine months to write and three years to sell," Wardlaw later recalled. "And that was fast. They say it can take seven years to break into the children's book market."*

Corey's Fire

Wardlaw's first full-length novel for middle-grade readers and young adults was *Corey's Fire,* a story based on the fire at her childhood home. To prepare to write the novel, she did research by interviewing family and friends and reading many news accounts. "Reliving the fire was painful," she said, "so painful that I was unable to begin writing the book until March of 1982, five years after the disaster." She quit teaching to finish the book.

After finishing the novel, she went looking for a publisher. "The book took nine months to write and three years to sell," Wardlaw later recalled. "And that was fast. They say it can take seven years to break into the children's book market." Still, her struggle wasn't over. She hoped the book would be published in 1987, which was the 10th anniversary of the fire. But the pub-

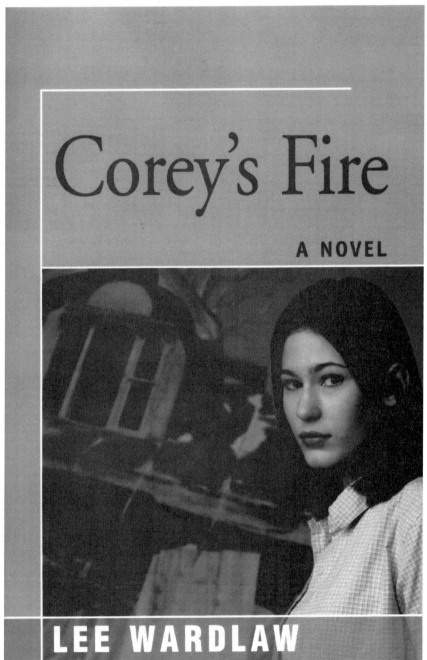

Corey's Fire

A NOVEL

LEE WARDLAW

Corey's Fire *was Wardlaw's first young adult novel.*

lishing company appointed a new editor for the project, and the editor hated it. Wardlaw had to find a new publisher, and the book didn't come out until 1990.

Corey's Fire (1990) tells the story of an immature 14-year-old girl who thinks no one understands her problems. Her deepening relationship with a neighbor, Christopher (Topher), is the center of the novel. At first, she can't stand him. Topher is sarcastic and likes to chase Corey's cat with his motorcycle. After her house burns down in a fire, however, it is Topher who helps her look for her cat and work through her problems. Another neighbor, Ericka, is also sympathetic, and eventually Corey begins to think about people other than herself. "It's not the disaster that changes Corey," Wardlaw explained. "She chooses to change. That's her first step to becoming an independent young woman."

Corey's Fire is dedicated to Wardlaw's mother and two brothers, who lived through the Santa Barbara fire with her. The book was well received by *Publishers Weekly*, where a critic wrote: "In this refreshing twist on the standard love story, romantic problems are upstaged by a natural disaster.... Corey finds the strength to rebuild her home and her life. The author's unflinching realism in describing the fire and its aftermath adds sizzle to an already appealing romance."

Other Fiction for Young Adults and Middle-Grade Readers

Wardlaw's writing career took off as she published book after book for various age groups. These included two novels for young adults: *Alley Cat* (1987) and *Don't Look Back* (1993). In *Alley Cat*, she relies on her own teenage experiences to tell the story of Allison Blake. Though initially awkward, Allison wins respect through her job as a weekend disk jockey at a radio station. In *Don't Look Back*, Wardlaw tells the story of 17-year-old Drew. Her father abandoned her and her mother and moved to Hawaii, for which she has never forgiven him. Now Drew is gong to spend the summer in Hawaii with him and his friend Jane. According to *Publishers Weekly*, "Drew has been afraid of flying, heights, and romantic relationships ever since her doctor father walked out on her family to start a new life in Hawaii. The unhappy girl must face her phobias when she spends the summer with the man she has grown to despise.... [Wardlaw] once again combines coming-of-age struggles with a predictable but pleasing romance."

Wardlaw has also written several books for middle-grade readers, including *Seventh Grade Weirdo*, published in 1992 and later released as *My Life as a Weirdo*. This novel tells the story of Christopher "Rob" Robin, whose family causes him major embarrassments. His mother, a Winnie-the-Pooh fanatic, drives around in a shocking pink van with Pooh characters on it; his father is an ex-surfer who likes to talk "surfer dude" slang around Rob's friends; and his sister, Winnie, is a six-year-old genius who is famous for inventing a board game. Rob wants nothing more than to be considered normal when he starts junior high school. But, of course, his "weird" family interferes with his plan, and Rob has the additional problem of dealing with a school bully. According to a reviewer for *VOYA (Voice of Youth Advocates)*, *Seventh Grade Weirdo* "humorously recounts the trials and tribulations of Rob's first year in junior high.... Wardlaw unerringly hits upon one of the chief fears of this age group: to be thought weird by their peers. Her light touch keeps a smile on your lips as you read. Sections cry out to be read aloud to classes, especially at the beginning of a new school year." The reviewer for the *Houston Chronicle* specifically recommended the book "for those entering the cutthroat social whirl of middle school or junior high."

—— " ——

Wardlaw knew she wanted to be a children's author, she explained, because "I have total recall of my childhood, not just what I did, but the emotions I felt. Childhood is a series of firsts and the wonder, the embarrassments, the traumas, and the tribulations are timeless. If you can remember what it felt like when you were a kid, you can connect with the kids of today."

—— " ——

Non-Fiction Books

Wardlaw has also written several non-fiction books for middle-grade and young adult readers. *Cowabunga! The Complete Book of Surfing* (1991) tells the history of surfing, recounts how the different kinds of surfboards were developed, and describes the movies, music, and slang associated with the sport. The book does not offer an instructional guide for beginners who want to learn to surf. "I'm not a great surfer," Wardlaw said. "I didn't feel I should teach kids how to do it." But there is a chapter on avoiding shark attacks, which includes this tip: paint two mean-looking eyes on the bottom of the board.

Bubblemania: The Chewy History of Bubble Gum (1997) is full of facts and off-beat trivia about bubble gum. It includes tips on how to blow huge gum bubbles, as well as a gum recipe suitable for an entire class to try. There is also a section on what Wardlaw calls "damage control: how to get gum off clothes, furniture, and hair—and how not to get it stuck there in the first place!"

Wardlaw and her pet cockroach, Toto, encourage kids to "catch the reading bug" at a presentation to young readers.

We All Scream for Ice Cream! The Scoop on America's Favorite Dessert (2000) is another favorite. To research and write the book, Wardlaw toured a dairy farm and two ice cream factories, interviewed taste testers, took scoop lessons, made ice cream, cones, and chocolate sauces in her kitchen, and gained six pounds tasting every brand of ice cream she could find. The result is a jam-packed book full of ice cream history, lore, licking tips, recipes, and more.

101 Ways to Bug Your Parents

One of Wardlaw's best-loved books is the middle-grade novel *101 Ways to Bug Your Parents* (1996). She got the idea for the book when a local California newspaper featured a story about a third grade teacher who gave her students an offbeat assignment—write down 10 things you've done that have really bugged your parents. The children began writing copiously, compiled a long list of their favorites, and wrote them on the blackboard. A teacher's aide thought the list was funny, and she copied it and sent it to the newspaper.

101 Ways to Bug Your Parents *has been a big hit with middle-school readers.*

Intrigued by the story, Wardlaw arranged to meet the California teacher, Nancy Revlin, and her class. Revlin was a first-year teacher who was worried that she would be fired due to the publicity from the news story and the negative letters the newspaper later received from irate parents. However, the principal saw the humor in the situation and supported her. But the incident tweaked Wardlaw's imagination, and she began to develop characters and a fictional storyline to go along with the list.

101 Ways to Bug Your Parents tells the story of Sneeze (Steve) Wyatt, a 12-year-old inventor whose latest invention is the Nice Alarm, which taps a person awake gently—when it works properly. Sneeze has written to a manufacturing company about his gadget, and the president of the company offers to meet him during the annual Invention Convention in July. He figures he'll be able to keep the appointment during his family's summer vacation, which is near the convention. But then his parents, unaware of his plans, cancel the vacation at the last minute and sign him up for a summer school creative-writing class. Frustrated and disappointed, Sneeze starts making a list of ways to annoy his parents. Some of his friends hear about the list, think he's writing a book on the subject, and want to buy copies.

——— **"** ———

"I think the parents who complained [about **101 Ways to Bug Your Parents***] don't have much of a sense of humor, which is something you need today if you're going to raise children,"* Wardlaw said. *"Of course, none of these parents actually took the time to read the book. If they had, they would've seen that the book is actually very pro-parent."*

——— **"** ———

Steve compiles his list gradually as the novel progresses, but the full list of 101 ways to bug your parents is included at the end. The "suggestions" include such annoyances as: chew with your mouth open, turn on the hot water when your dad's in the shower, give your brother or sister a haircut, lose french fries under the car seat, repeat everything your parents say, make your parents come to school with the homework you "forgot," put clean clothes back in the hamper, don't flush the toilet, and say to your mom: "that's a woman's job."

101 Ways to Bug Your Parents found an enthusiastic audience among middle school readers, many of whom continue to write to Wardlaw with suggested additions to the list. The book was also well received by the literary

press. A critic for *School Library Journal* called the book "a fast, fun read. The humor and depth of the characters are reminiscent of Louis Sachar's *There's a Boy in the Girls' Bathroom*. Readers will hope for further adventures of Sneeze and his friends." According to a reviewer for *Booklist*, "Wardlaw has written a funny story with more substance than is evident initially. The death of a parent, job insecurity, gifted children, teacher respect, true friendship, and even intellectual freedom all find play here. Although adults may find Sneeze's suggestions predictable and overdone—after all, we've weighed in on both sides of this issue—children will probably continue to turn the pages just to see whether they've overlooked even one idea." *101 Ways to Bug Your Parents* was a great success: it won several awards, became a perennial favorite among readers, and was optioned for a movie on the Disney Channel.

101 Ways to Bug Your Parents sparked some controversy, however, especially among parents who worried their children would take the book to heart and use it as an instructional manual. Parents in two school districts in Texas and Oklahoma went so far as to challenge the book and ask that it be removed from school shelves. They felt the book undermined parental authority and encouraged children to disobey. In both cases, members of the school board read the book and then denied the requests.

"I think the parents who complained don't have much of a sense of humor, which is something you need today if you're going to raise children," Wardlaw said. "Of course, none of these parents actually took the time to read the book. If they had, they would've seen that the book is actually very pro-parent, and that Sneeze learns that bugging your parents not only gets you into real trouble, but that it's an ineffective and improper means of communicating with your mom and dad."

101 Ways to Bug Your Teacher

Several years later, Wardlaw followed up with the sequel, *101 Ways to Bug Your Teacher* (2004). This book features the same main characters, Sneeze Wyatt and his friends at Jefferson Middle School. This time Sneeze's problem is his parents' desire for him to take advanced math and science classes. They want him to skip a grade and go straight into high school at the end of seventh grade. Sneeze is horrified by the idea of skipping eighth grade, mostly because he'd miss his friends. So he sets out to prove that he's not high-school material by becoming disruptive in his classes. He makes a list of 101 ways to bug his teachers, with the hope that they will recommend that he stay in middle school.

> *Wardlaw has said that these two suggestions from* **101 Ways to Bug Your Teachers** *used to drive her crazy. Number 13: "While the teacher is talking, get up to grind your pencil. Grind loudly." And Number 33: "When a teacher asks a question, wave your arm like a palm tree in a hurricane and say: 'Pick me! Pick me!' When the teacher calls on you, say: 'Never mind.'"*

Most of the ideas on the list were contributed by real students, with others added by Wardlaw, drawing on her days as a teacher. "Number 13 and 33 [on the list] used to drive me crazy!" she said. Number 13: "While the teacher is talking, get up to grind your pencil. Grind loudly." And Number 33: "When a teacher asks a question, wave your arm like a palm tree in a hurricane and say: 'Pick me! Pick me!' When the teacher calls on you, say: 'Never mind.'"

101 Ways to Bug Your Teacher has several subplots, including the pregnancy of Sneeze's mother and his friend Hayley's difficulties with the woman dating her widowed father. There is also a story line about the group project that Sneeze and his friends have to prepare for their class in ancient Egyptian history. After some initial reluctance, the group decides to go ahead with Sneeze's idea to make a mummy out of a chicken. Wardlaw

177

ends *101 Ways to Bug Your Teacher* with a three-page, 21-step recipe for making a mummy out of a store-bought chicken!

Most reviewers of *101 Ways to Bug Your Teacher* praised the book, including this comment in *School Library Journal:* "References are made to the first book, but this one can stand alone. In spite of the title, the characters show respect for their teachers and parents, and for one another. A delightful read." A *Booklist* reviewer agreed. "Sneeze is an appealing, dimensional character whose first-person narrative is bound to entertain. The story is both comical and compassionate as it highlights the challenges of living up to expectations and the rewards of trying your best."

——— " ———

Wardlaw plans to continue to write because "It's fun.... First and foremost, I write to entertain myself. But I also write to show my readers a world they can delight in, a world of wonder and awe, a world where so much is possible. Around any bend, at any moment, might come Mystery! Adventure! Romance!"

——— " ———

Wardlaw has been working on two additional sequels to the series, tentatively titled *101 Ways to Bug Your Brother or Sister* and *101 Ways to Bug Your Friends and Enemies*. She invites her readers to offer suggestions on their "bugging" techniques by clicking on the "Just for Kids" icon on her website.

Wardlaw plans to continue to write because "It's fun.... First and foremost, I write to entertain myself. But I also write to show my readers a world they can delight in, a world of wonder and awe, a world where so much is possible. Around any bend, at any moment, might come Mystery! Adventure! Romance!"

MARRIAGE AND FAMILY

Wardlaw married Craig Jaffurs in 1983. They are the co-owners of Jaffurs Wine Cellars, which makes about 5,000 cases of wine a year from grapes purchased from vineyards in Santa Barbara, California. The couple lives in Santa Barbara with their son, Patterson, who was born in 1996. The family has two cats.

HOBBIES AND OTHER INTERESTS

When she's not writing, Wardlaw has many favorite activities, which she listed on her website as: "crossword puzzles; reading history (American Revolutionary and Civil War eras); body-surfing; hanging out with my son;

baking (and eating) anything with dark chocolate; shopping with friends; blowing bubble gum bubbles; collecting beach glass; and visiting schools to talk to kids about writing." In addition to her work with children, she also teaches workshops for adult writers, parents, librarians, and teachers. Wardlaw writes daily blogs on her lively and kid-friendly website.

SELECTED WRITINGS

Fiction for Young Adults

Alley Cat, 1987
Don't Look Back, 1993
See You in September, 1995 (collection of stories by Wardlaw and three other authors)

Fiction for Middle-Grade Readers

Corey's Fire, 1990
Operation Rhinoceros, 1992
Seventh Grade Weirdo, 1992; later released as *My Life as a Weirdo*
101 Ways to Bug Your Parents, 1996
101 Ways to Bug Your Teacher, 2004
Tripping Over the Lunch Lady and Other School Stories, 2004 (collection of stories by Wardlaw and nine other authors)

Non-Fiction

Cowabunga! The Complete Book of Surfing, 1991
Bubblemania: The Chewy History of Bubble Gum, 1997
We All Scream for Ice Cream! The Scoop on America's Favorite Dessert, 2000

Easy Readers and Beginning Chapter Books

Me + Math = Headache, 1986
The Eye and I, 1988
The Ghoul Brothers, 1996
Dinosaur Pizza, 1998
Hector's Hiccups, 1999

Picture Books

The Tales of Grandpa Cat, 1994
Punia and the King of Shark: A Hawaiian Folktale, 1997

An illustration of Wardlaw by Cathi Mingus.

Bow-Wow Birthday, 1998
First Steps, 1999
Saturday Night Jamboree, 2000
The Chair Where Bear Sits, 2001
*Peek-a-Book: A Lift-the-Flap Bedtime
  Rhyme*, 2003

SELECTED HONORS
AND AWARDS

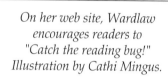

Reluctant Young Adult Reader Award
  (American Library Association):
  1991, for *Corey's Fire;* 1992, for
  Cowabunga

*On her web site, Wardlaw
encourages readers to
"Catch the reading bug!"
Illustration by Cathi Mingus.*

Children's Choice Award (Interna-
  tional Reading Association/Chil-
  dren's Book Council): 1991, for
  Corey's Fire; 2005 (two awards), for *101 Ways to Bug Your Teacher* and *Trip-
  ping Over the Lunch Lady and Other School Stories*
Santa Barbara High School Distinguished Alumni Award: 1993, for suc-
  cess as a children's book author
Pick of the Lists Award (American Booksellers): 1994, for *The Tales of
  Grandpa Cat;* 1996, for *101 Ways to Bug Your Parents*
Best Books for the Teen Age Award (New York Public Library): 1996, for *See
  You in September*
Notable Children's Book in the Field of Social Studies (Children's Book
  Council/National Council for the Social Studies): 1998, for *Punia and the
  King of Sharks*
100 of the Decade's Best Multi-Cultural Read Alouds (Reading Is Funda-
  mental): 1998, for *Punia and the King of Sharks*
Best Children's Books of the Year Award (Bank Street College): 2000, for
  First Steps; 2001, for *Saturday Night Jamboree*
Best Humorous Books of the Year Award (Bank Street College): 2001, for
  101 Ways to Bug Your Parents
International School Librarians Recommended Reading List: 2004, for *101
  Ways to Bug Your Parents*
Shojai Mentor Award (International Cat Writers' Association): 2005

FURTHER READING

Periodicals

Daily Oklahoman, May 10, 2000, Community section, p.1
Fresno (CA) Bee, Mar. 19, 1995, p.J8

Los Angeles Times, Aug. 1, 1991, p.J14; July 6, 2000, p.B9; June 25, 2003, Food
section, p.7
New England Reading Association Journal, Vol.37, No.3, 2001, p.14
Santa Barbara News-Press, Dec. 10, 2003

Online Articles

http://www.californiareaders.org/interviews/wardlaw_lee.php
(*California Readers*, "Meet Lee Wardlaw," no date)
http://patriciamnewman.com/wardlaw.html
(*Patricia M. Newman*, "Who Wrote That? Featuring Lee Wardlaw," originally published in *California Kids!* June 2002)

ADDRESS

Lee Wardlaw
c/o Ms. Ginger Knowlton
Curtis Brown, Ltd.
Ten Astor Place
New York, NY 10003
Email: author@leewardlaw.com

WORLD WIDE WEB SITE

http://www.leewardlaw.com

Photo and Illustration Credits

Front Cover Photos: Carter: James Burling Chase, courtesy of Sustainable South Bronx; Gomez: Fitzroy Barrett/Landov; Gore: Joel Ryan/PA Photos/Landov; Perry: HOUSE OF PAYNE. Copyright © Turner Broadcasting System, Inc. Photo by Alfeo Dixon.

Aly & AJ/Photos: Todd Williamson/WireImage for Elizabeth Glaser Pediatric AIDS (p. 9); John M. Heller/Getty Images (p. 12); CD: INTO THE RUSH. Copyright © & p 2005 Hollywood Records, Inc. All rights reserved. Photo by Keith Munyan. (p. 15 top); DVD: COW BELLES © Disney. All rights reserved. (p. 15 bottom); CD: INSOMNIATIC. Copyright © & p 2007 Hollywood Records, Inc. All rights reserved. (p. 16).

Majora Carter/Photos: MacArthur Foundation (pp. 21, 30); James Burling Chase (pp. 24, 26, 28). All photos are courtesy of Sustainable South Bronx.

Anderson Cooper/Photos: Jason Kempin/WireImage (p. 33); Susan Wood/Getty Images (p. 35); Courtesy, Yale University (p. 38); lm1/Zuma Press/Newscom (p. 41); Charlie Varley/Sipa Press/Newscom (p.43); DISPATCHES FROM THE EDGE © 2006 by Anderson Cooper. All rights reserved. Published by HarperCollins. Photograph by Brent Stirton/Getty Images for CNN; jacket design by Chip Kidd (p. 45).

Selena Gomez/Photos: Fitzroy Barrett/Landov (p. 49); BARNEY & FRIENDS. HIT Entertainment, The Lyons Group/Connecticut Public Television. All rights reserved. (p. 51); DVD: WIZARDS OF WAVERLY PLACE: WIZARD SCHOOL © Disney. All rights reserved. (p. 54); DR. SEUSS' HORTON HEARS A WHO! TM © 2008 Twentieth Century Fox Film Corporation. Photo by Blue Sky Studios. Dr. Seuss, Horton Hears a Who! and Dr. Seuss Characters TM & © 1954, 2008 Dr. Seuss Enterprises, L.P. All rights reserved. (p. 56).

Al Gore/Photos: Junko Kimura/Getty Images (p. 59); AP Photo (p. 62); Jeffrey Markowitz/ Sygma/Corbis (p. 64); Marilyn Weiss/AP Photo (p. 66); William J. Clinton Presidential Library (p. 68); Luke Frazza/AFP/Getty Images (p. 71); AN INCONVENIENT TRUTH by Al Gore, © Al Gore, 2006, 2007. Adapted for young readers by Jane O'-Connor. Published by Viking/Penguin/Rodale, Inc. Photo of Al Gore © Eric Lee/Renewable Films, front cover photo courtesy of NASA, jacket design by Jim Hoover. (p. 74); Daniel Sannum Lauten/AFP/Getty Images (p. 77).

Eli Manning/Photos: Al Bello/Getty Images (p. 81); Courtesy of Ole Miss Athletics (pp. 83, 87); Ray Stubblebine/Reuters/Landov (p. 89); Andy Lyons/Getty Images (p. 92); Mike Groll/AP Photo (p. 94).

Cumulative Names Index

This cumulative index includes the names of all individuals profiled in *Biography Today* since the debut of the series in 1992.

For cumulative general, places of birth, and birthday indexes, please see biographytoday.com.

185

For cumulative general, places of birth, and birthday indexes, please see biographytoday.com.

For cumulative general, places of birth, and birthday indexes, please see biographytoday.com.

187

For cumulative general, places of birth, and birthday indexes, please see biographytoday.com.

191

For cumulative general, places of birth, and birthday indexes, please see biographytoday.com.

For cumulative general, places of birth, and birthday indexes, please see biographytoday.com.

For cumulative general, places of birth, and birthday indexes, please see biographytoday.com.

For cumulative general, places of birth, and birthday indexes, please see biographytoday.com.

199

Biography Today

General Series

For ages 9 and above

Biography Today **General Series** includes a unique combination of current biographical profiles that teachers and librarians — and the readers themselves — tell us are most appealing. The **General Series** is available as a 3-issue subscription; hardcover annual cumulation; or subscription plus cumulation.

Within the **General Series**, your readers will find a variety of sketches about:

- Authors
- Musicians
- Political leaders
- Sports figures
- Movie actresses & actors
- Cartoonists
- Scientists
- Astronauts
- TV personalities
- and the movers & shakers in many other fields!

"Biography Today will be useful in elementary and middle school libraries and in public library children's collections where there is a need for biographies of current personalities. High schools serving reluctant readers may also want to consider a subscription."
— *Booklist,* American Library Association

"Highly recommended for the young adult audience. Readers will delight in the accessible, energetic, tell-all style; teachers, librarians, and parents will welcome the clever format [and] intelligent and informative text. It should prove especially useful in motivating 'reluctant' readers or literate nonreaders."
— *MultiCultural Review*

"Written in a friendly, almost chatty tone, the profiles offer quick, objective information. While coverage of current figures makes *Biography Today* **a useful reference tool, an appealing format and wide scope make it a fun resource to browse."** — *School Library Journal*

"The best source for current information at a level kids can understand."
— Kelly Bryant, School Librarian, Carlton, OR

"Easy for kids to read. We love it! Don't want to be without it."
— Lynn McWhirter, School Librarian, Rockford, IL

ONE-YEAR SUBSCRIPTION
- 3 softcover issues, 6" x 9"
- Published in January, April, and September
- 1-year subscription, list price $66. **School and library price $64**
- 150 pages per issue
- 10 profiles per issue
- Contact sources for additional information
- Cumulative Names Index

HARDBOUND ANNUAL CUMULATION
- Sturdy 6" x 9" hardbound volume
- Published in December
- List price $73. **School and library price $66 per volume**
- 450 pages per volume
- 30 profiles — includes all profiles found in softcover issues for that calendar year
- Cumulative General Index, Places of Birth Index, and Birthday Index

SUBSCRIPTION AND CUMULATION COMBINATION
- $110 for 3 softcover issues plus the hardbound volume

For Cumulative General, Places of Birth, and Birthday Indexes, please see www.biographytoday.com.